✧ *Companions for the Journey* ✧

Praying with
Anthony of Padua

✧ *Companions for the Journey* ✧

Praying with Anthony of Padua

by
Madeline Pecora Nugent

Saint Mary's Press
Christian Brothers Publications
Winona, Minnesota

✧ *To Claude Jarmak, OFM Conv.,* ✧
whose translations of Anthony's sermon notes
have made the saint's spirituality available
to the English-speaking world

The publishing team for this book included Carl Koch, development editor; Laurie Berg Rohda, manuscript editor; Maura C. Goessling, typesetter; Elaine Kohner, illustrator; Maurine R. Twait, cover designer and art director; pre-press, printing, and binding by the graphics division of Saint Mary's Press.

The acknowledgments continue on page 117.

Printed in the United States of America

Printing: 9 8 7 6 5 4 3 2 1

Year: 2004 03 02 01 00 99 98 97 96

ISBN 0-88489-397-9

✧ Contents ✧

✧ Foreword ✧

Companions for the Journey

Just as food is required for human life, so are companions. Indeed, the word *companions* comes from two Latin words: *com*, meaning "with," and *panis*, meaning "bread." Companions nourish our heart, mind, soul, and body. They are also the people with whom we can celebrate the sharing of bread.

Perhaps the most touching stories in the Bible are about companionship: the Last Supper, the wedding feast at Cana, the sharing of the loaves and the fishes, and Jesus' breaking of bread with the disciples on the road to Emmaus. Each incident of companionship with Jesus revealed more about his mercy, love, wisdom, suffering, and hope. When Jesus went to pray in the Garden of Olives, he craved the companionship of the Apostles. They let him down. But God sent the Spirit to inflame the hearts of the Apostles, and they became faithful companions to Jesus and to one another.

Throughout history, other faithful companions have followed Jesus and the Apostles. These saints and mystics have also taken the journey from conversion, through suffering, to resurrection. Just as they were inspired by the holy people who went before them, so too may you be inspired by these saints and mystics and take them as your companions on your spiritual journey.

The Companions for the Journey series is a response to the spiritual hunger of Christians. This series makes available the rich spiritual teachings of mystics and guides whose wisdom can help us on our pilgrimage. As you complete the last meditation in each volume, it is hoped that you will feel supported, challenged, and affirmed by a soul-companion on your spiritual journey.

The spiritual hunger that has emerged over the last twenty years is a great sign of renewal in Christian life. People fill retreat programs and workshops on topics in spirituality. The demand for spiritual directors exceeds the number available. Interest in the lives and writings of saints and mystics is increasing as people search for models of whole and holy Christian life.

Praying with Anthony

Praying with Anthony of Padua is more than just a book about Anthony's spirituality. This book seeks to engage you in praying in the way that Anthony did about issues and themes that were central to his experience. Each meditation can enlighten your understanding of his spirituality and lead you to reflect on your own experience.

The goal of *Praying with Anthony of Padua* is that you will discover Anthony's rich spirituality and integrate his spirit and wisdom into your relationship with God, with your brothers and sisters, and with your own heart and mind.

Suggestions for Praying with Anthony

Meet Anthony of Padua, a fascinating companion for your pilgrimage, by reading the introduction to this book. It provides a brief biography of Anthony and an outline of the major themes of his spirituality.

Once you meet Anthony, you will be ready to pray with him and to encounter God, your sisters and brothers, and yourself in new and wonderful ways. To help your prayer, here are some suggestions that have been part of the tradition of Christian spirituality:

Create a sacred space. Jesus said, "'Whenever you pray, go into your room and shut the door and pray to your [God] who is in secret; and your [God] who sees in secret will reward you'" (Matthew 6:6). Solitary prayer is best done in a place where you can have privacy and silence, both of which can be luxuries in the life of busy people. If privacy and silence are not possible, create a quiet, safe place within yourself, perhaps while riding to and from work, while sitting in line at the dentist's office, or while waiting for someone. Do the best you can, knowing that a loving God is present everywhere. Whether the meditations in this book are used for solitary prayer or with a group, try to create a prayerful mood with candles, meditative music, an open Bible, or a crucifix.

Open yourself to the power of prayer. Every human experience has a religious dimension. All of life is suffused with God's presence. So remind yourself that God is present as you begin your period of prayer. Do not worry about distractions. If something keeps intruding during your prayer, spend some time talking with God about it. Be flexible because God's Spirit blows where it will.

Prayer can open your mind and widen your vision. Be open to new ways of seeing God, people, and yourself. As you open yourself to the Spirit of God, different emotions are evoked, such as sadness from tender memories, or joy from a celebration recalled. Our emotions are messages from God that can tell us much about our spiritual quest. Also, prayer strengthens our will to act. Through prayer, God can touch our will and empower us to live according to what we know is true.

Finally, many of the meditations in this book will call you to employ your memories, your imagination, and the circumstances of your life as subjects for prayer. The great mystics and saints realized that they had to use all their resources to know God better. Indeed, God speaks to us continually and touches us constantly. We must learn to listen and feel with all the means that God has given us.

Come to prayer with an open mind, heart, and will.

Preview each meditation before beginning. After you have placed yourself in God's presence, spend a few moments previewing the readings and especially the reflection activities. Several reflection activities are given in each meditation because different styles of prayer appeal to different personalities or personal needs. **Note that each meditation has more**

reflection activities than can be done during one prayer period. Therefore, select only one or two reflection activities each time you use a meditation. Do not feel compelled to complete all the reflection activities.

Read meditatively. Each meditation offers you a story about Anthony and a reading from his writings. Take your time reading. If a particular phrase touches you, stay with it. Relish its feelings, meanings, and concerns.

Use the reflections. Following the readings is a short reflection in commentary form, which is meant to give perspective to the readings. Then you are offered several ways of meditating on the readings and the theme of the prayer. You may be familiar with the different methods of meditating, but in case you are not, they are described briefly here:

✦ *Repeated short prayer or mantra:* One means of focusing your prayer is to use a *mantra,* or "prayer word." The mantra may be a single word or a short phrase taken from the readings or from the Scriptures. For example, a short prayer for meditation 3 in this book might simply be the name of Jesus. Repeated slowly in harmony with your breathing, the mantra helps you center your heart and mind on one action or attribute of God.

✦ *Lectio divina:* This type of meditation is "divine studying," a concentrated reflection on the word of God or the wisdom of a spiritual writer. Most often in *lectio divina,* you will be invited to read one of the passages several times and then concentrate on one or two sentences, pondering their meaning for you and their effect on you. *Lectio divina* commonly ends with formulation of a resolution.

✦ *Guided meditation:* In this type of meditation, our imagination helps us consider alternative actions and likely consequences. Our imagination helps us experience new ways of seeing God, our neighbors, ourselves, and nature. When Jesus told his followers parables and stories, he engaged their imagination. In this book, you will be invited to follow guided meditations.

One way of doing a guided meditation is to read the scene or story several times, until you know the outline and can recall it when you enter into reflection. Or before your prayer time, you may wish to record the meditation on a tape recorder. If so, remember to allow pauses for reflection between phrases and to speak with a slow, peaceful pace and tone. Then, during prayer, when you have finished the readings and the reflection commentary, you can turn on your recording of the meditation and be led through it. If you find your own voice too distracting, ask a friend to make the tape for you.

✦ *Examen of consciousness:* The reflections often will ask you to examine how God has been speaking to you in your past and present experience—in other words, the reflections will ask you to examine your awareness of God's presence in your life.

✦ *Journal writing:* Writing is a process of discovery. If you write for any length of time, stating honestly what is on your mind and in your heart, you will unearth much about who you are, how you stand with your God, what deep longings reside in your soul, and more. In some reflections you will be asked to write a dialog with Jesus or someone else. If you have never used writing as a means of meditation, try it. Reserve a special notebook for your journal writing. If desired, you can go back to your entries at a future time for an examen of consciousness.

✦ *Action:* Occasionally, a reflection will suggest singing a favorite hymn, going out for a walk, or undertaking some other physical activity. Actions can be meaningful forms of prayer.

Using the Meditations for Group Prayer

If you wish to use the meditations for community prayer, these suggestions may help:

✦ Read the theme to the group. Call the community into the presence of God, using the short opening prayer. Invite one or two participants to read one or both readings. If you use both readings, observe the pause between them.

✦ The reflection commentary may be used as a reading, or it can be deleted, depending on the needs and interests of the group.

✦ Select one of the reflection activities for your group. Allow sufficient time for your group to reflect, to recite a centering prayer or mantra, to accomplish a studying prayer *(lectio divina)*, or to finish an examen of consciousness. Depending on the group and the amount of time available, you may want to invite the participants to share their reflections, responses, or petitions with the group.

✦ Reading the passage from the Scriptures may serve as a summary of the meditation.

✦ If a formulated prayer or a psalm is given as a closing, it may be recited by the entire group. Or you may ask participants to offer their own prayers for the closing.

Now you are ready to begin praying with Anthony of Padua, a faithful and caring companion on this stage of your spiritual journey. It is hoped that you will find him to be a true soul-companion.

CARL KOCH
Editor

✧ Introduction ✧

More Than the Finder of Lost Objects

"Tony, Tony, come around
Something's lost that must be found."

Most people know Anthony of Padua as the saint who finds lost objects. But he is much more than that. He is the saint who finds lost souls and who seeks to return them to God, to whom all souls ultimately belong.

To Anthony, God was not an abstraction or a quality. God was a real, vibrant entity who took on human flesh and came to earth, and who still lives afresh in the world through the Holy Spirit. God was the goal of all living, the reason for existence, and the source of all love. To Anthony, the world of nature and humanity was precious and beautiful beyond all telling, but all creation put together could not begin to approximate the value of God, the pearl of great price. For Anthony, God was all in all. God was the creator and redeemer of all that existed. God was the love in all that existed.

A brilliant man, Anthony apparently had memorized the Bible. He possessed an amazing ability to apply the Scriptures to life and to tie together seemingly unrelated Scripture verses to make a point. Anthony often took seldom quoted Scripture verses and developed entire sermons from them. For Anthony, every word of the Scriptures pointed to one being, Jesus Christ.

The entire universe from the immense sun to the smallest gnat held lessons about God, if only one was willing to look for them. Even the letters in certain words and in the various names for God offered deep spiritual messages. Because of

Anthony's profound theological insights, evidenced by his preaching success and his written sermon notes, Pope Pius XII gave him the title doctor of the Gospel.

Anthony of Padua can teach us how to read the Scriptures and how to pray. But that is not all he can teach us. He can guide us in becoming acutely aware of God's presence in the world around us. He can paint for us the breathing picture of a living God in human flesh. He can coax us to eliminate the superfluous from our life and to grope for the core of existence, who is God alone. Praying with Anthony can help us experience the world, the Scriptures, and Christ himself in a richer way.

Praying with Anthony calls us to be the person whom God created us to be.

Problems with Anthony's History

Getting to the core of Anthony's story is difficult because so much discrepancy exists in the historical record. To start at the beginning, the very year of Anthony's birth is questionable. Although the date of his death, 13 June 1231, is certain, questions persist about the date of his birth. Earlier historians claimed that he was born in 1195, but carbon dating of his remains puts his birth four or five years earlier.

Was Anthony really the son of Martin de Bulhoes, a Portuguese knight, and his young wife, Maria Teresa, herself of noble background? Or were the details of nobility added to make Anthony's relinquishment of his past even more romantic and heroic than it would have been if he had been born into a common family?

Anthony preached in Italy and southern France, but exactly where he was at any particular time is questionable. Different cities and towns claim to be the location of the commonly told miracles and legends about him. Thus, three cities claim that within their city limits, Anthony caused a "beast of burden" (either a mare, horse, or mule, depending on the story) to adore the Eucharist.

At least five places in France and Italy state that Anthony was seen there holding the Christ Child. Two French cities claim that a dual apparition took place within their precincts:

Anthony was seen simultaneously celebrating the Eucharist for the public and singing in a choir with other friars.

Legends tell that one of the popes heard Anthony preach and called him the "Ark of the Testament" and then declared that Anthony could rewrite the Bible from memory if the Scriptures were lost. But which of three popes was it?

Did Anthony, a member of the Friars Minor, ever meet Francis of Assisi? Did Francis send him to Rome on business of the order?

Which of the many miracles attributed to Anthony during his lifetime actually happened?

Popular legends about Anthony's life are influenced more by hagiographic tradition than historical record. Hagiography comes from two Greek words: *hagios*, meaning "holy," and *graphos*, meaning "writings." Hagiographers write with the intention of inspiring readers to faith and piety. They may choose or embellish incidents in order to emphasize certain points or to present a certain moral or theological view. While hagiographers write biography, they do so with a freedom that modern historical biographers shun. Legends, stories, and hearsay, if they touch on theological truths or inspire faith, can play just as important a role in hagiography as provable fact.

All this does not mean that hagiography is based on fantasy. On the contrary, many incidents in Anthony's life, as recorded by hagiographers, probably have a basis in fact. But readers need to keep in mind that they are reading more than strict biography; they are reading the hagiographer's moral lessons.

To a degree, readers must suspend their concern about the inconsistencies in Anthony's record. The legends do carry his spirit. Besides, some aspects of his life can be documented.

Anthony's Early Life

Anthony was born in Lisbon, Portugal, in the early 1190s. He was baptized Fernando. Between the ages of fifteen and twenty, Anthony felt increasingly disillusioned by worldly pursuits and asked to be admitted to Saint Vincent's Monastery, an Augustinian foundation in Lisbon. His father, disappointed that Anthony would not follow the career his family had planned for him, reluctantly gave his son permission to enter religious life. About a year later, Fernando, distracted by constant visits from his worldly friends and his family, asked for a transfer to a more distant monastery. He was sent to Holy Cross, a monastery in Coimbra, Portugal, about a hundred and twenty miles from Lisbon. Here he found the solitude that he sought.

In its day, Holy Cross was a famous center of learning. Fernando could very well have spent many hours in its library, pouring over numerous books on theology and natural science, and soaking up all that he read.

From Augustinian to Friar Minor

The prior at Coimbra recognized a certain charisma and charm about this young monk and so made him the guest master. In this capacity, Fernando greeted all classes of people who came to the monastery, from the queen of Portugal herself to the poorest leper looking for alms. Frequently friars from the new order founded by Francis Bernardone of Assisi, Italy, came begging at Holy Cross. Fernando grew to like these poor but joyful Friars Minor.

One day, five friars on their way to Morocco stopped at the monastery. They told Fernando that they were going to preach to the Moors and looked forward, with great happiness, to their martyrdom there. The courage, joy, and faith of these young men touched Fernando deeply.

Later, when their martyred remains were interred at Holy Cross, he prayed long hours at their reliquaries. Fernando began to discern a call. God wanted his life, and he could only give it, he thought, by becoming a martyr. To do this, he would have to go to Morocco. To go to Morocco, he would have to become a Franciscan friar, for the Augustinians were attached to their monasteries for life.

So Fernando asked the Franciscans to accept him on the condition that they send him to Morocco. They agreed. Somehow he received permission to follow his calling from all the monks at Holy Cross. After being clothed in the gray woolen tunic of the followers of Francis, Fernando was renamed Anthony, after Anthony of the Desert, the patron saint of the Franciscan hermitage outside of Coimbra.

Shortly after his investiture, Anthony sailed to Morocco and to what he thought would be his destiny as a martyr, but he never got a chance to preach there. Struck with a fever so severe that he was prostrate for months, he finally decided to return to Portugal to regain his health. However, the ship on which he sailed encountered a violent gale that blew it to the shores of Sicily, where it ran aground.

Anthony was taken to a Franciscan monastery and then, some months later, to Assisi for a chapter meeting of the entire order. At this meeting, a provincial of the order assigned Anthony to a small hermitage in the mountains outside of Forli, Italy. Anthony replied that he would do whatever he was told.

In the solitude of a small cave at the hermitage of Monte Paolo, Anthony wrote of his thoughts and prayed for long hours. In his desire to subjugate his bodily needs and passions to his goal of union with Christ, he followed the pattern of many holy people of his time. He fasted and disciplined his body. His fervor was so intense that he sometimes fainted on the way to his meals and so was told by the monastery's guardian to lessen his severity. This he did. So as to be of some help to the brothers, Anthony cooked and cleaned in the kitchen.

Thrust into the Public Arena

In March of 1222, an ordination of some Franciscans and Dominicans was to take place at Forli. The guardian of Monte Paolo attended this ordination, and Anthony went along. Historians disagree on whether Anthony was ordained a priest at this time or while he was an Augustinian.

Following the ordination and a meal, an embarrassing situation arose. Whoever was supposed to arrange for a speaker had not done his job. In the presence of the bishop, one friar after another declined to speak, each pleading that he was not prepared to talk. Finally, the provincial asked Anthony, who had once said, "I will do whatever you tell me." Anthony was told to preach under obedience as the Holy Spirit directed and to take as his text, "Christ became obedient unto death, even to death on a cross."

A bit hesitantly, Anthony began to speak. Then his preaching gained more force. His deep knowledge of the Scriptures, history, and natural science bubbled forth in amazing analogies. His long hours of prayer and contemplation flowed through his words, and his listeners felt themselves drawn into the very mystery and beauty of God. When Anthony concluded his talk, a wave of awe swept the crowd. As a result, the friar with dishpan hands was sent to preach to the people.

Mission to the Cathars

In Anthony's day, the church was in a mortal struggle with a sect known as the Cathars, or Albigensians, named after the town Albi, the Cathars' stronghold in southern France. The Cathars claimed that all matter was evil and created by Satan and that only the world of the spirit, which was the creation of the good God, was good. Since flesh was evil, Christ could not have come as a human being.

According to the Cathars, physical life by its nature was sinful, so reproduction was even more sinful. Thus, consummation in marriage damned the couple. Some Cathar preachers taught that the proper way to be freed from life, which was itself evil, was to commit suicide. A strict minority group called themselves the "Perfect Ones." Only those who believed the Catharist teachings were assured of eternal salvation. All others were condemned to endless cycles of death and rebirth until they, too, came to see the wisdom of the heresy and embraced the Catharist faith.

The church was losing its battle with the Cathars in large part because of its clergy. Holy Catholic priests were rare. Many of the clergy were lax and self-indulgent. Frequently they scandalized the faithful with their public sins of sexual license, sexual abuse, usury, and drunkenness. Many clerics knew very little of the Scriptures. Few actually preached.

The people, hungry for spiritual guidance and hope, understandably felt frustrated with the Catholic church. More and more they turned to Catharist preachers, who were not living in sin and whose lives clearly modeled austerity, compassion, and faith. People who had never heard their parish priest give a scriptural homily now heard preachers in the streets quoting the Scriptures freely and with great knowledge, applying the Scriptures to life and using them to illustrate their own doctrines. Some families had been Cathars for generations, but now more and more people were converting. Some French and Italian cities were nearly all made up of Cathars.

Why was the church so upset over this religious aberration? In truth, the Catharist heresy contained distortions of the Good News. Like most heresies, Catharism took to extremes a positive impulse for renewal. Heresies throughout Christian history have often begun as correctives for church practices that needed to be challenged. But renewal becomes heresy when it denies some essential aspect of the faith—in this case, the Incarnation of Jesus, the goodness of creation, and the sacredness of human life.

For more than fifty years church leaders had tolerated or ignored the Cathars. When their influence began to spread more widely, popes sent the Franciscans and Dominicans to them.

Anthony as Evangelist

Into this charged atmosphere came Anthony. The Cathars went barefoot and lived in poverty. Like his brother friars, so did Anthony. The heretics quoted the Scriptures and knew the Bible. So did Anthony. The heretics were compassionate and helpful. So was Anthony.

Anthony did not enter into public debates with the Cathars. Rather, he preached the Catholic faith by his own applications of the Scriptures. Anthony's goal seemed to be this: teach the people about the richness of their faith, and they will see the truth of it.

Anthony was trained in the Augustinian method of interpreting the Scriptures. He began by spending time each day in reading *(lectio divina)*, contemplating *(meditatio)*, and praying over the Scriptures *(ruminatio)*. The *meditatio* was actually a form of memorization in which Anthony would read the text orally to imprint it on his mind. In the *ruminatio*, he would mentally review the text again and again, drawing out from it every facet of meaning. Thus, Anthony's sermons *(oratio)* were the fruit of many hours spent alone with God's word and Spirit.

When Anthony was ready to preach, he would first select a verse and give its literal meaning. Then he would progress to its spiritual or symbolic meaning. He would analyze the verse, looking at phrases, words, and sometimes the very letters in words, drawing analogies from them and bringing in other scriptural verses and writings of church theologians and philosophers, until an entire message was fleshed out. In doing this, he used his knowledge of natural phenomena, as was taught at the time, as well as examples from the world around him.

Because the emperor was bringing many exotic animals into the empire, the people were fascinated by lions, leopards, elephants, monkeys, and rhinoceroses. Anthony used all these animals and more in his sermons. When Anthony mentioned one of these creatures, his audience immediately became attentive, just as we might become immediately attentive if a speaker uses a well-known celebrity as an example.

Anthony's technique often succeeded because his audiences could see that he was living fully every word that he preached. He was totally committed to God and brimming with joyful peace.

Ministry

Anthony stayed busy, but he always took time for whoever came to him for help or counsel. For Anthony, to serve humanity was to serve his Creator.

Besides being a preacher, Anthony was, at different times during the ten years that he was a Franciscan, custodian (local leader) of several friaries and provincial of the Romagna in Italy. He traveled frequently, always on foot.

In addition, Anthony was the first teacher of theology in the Franciscan order. He taught his brothers to approach the Scriptures through study and contemplation, and his influence on their preaching methods was profound. Saint Bonaventure and Venerable John Duns Scotus expanded upon

Anthony's method of interpreting the Scriptures and embraced the logic and disputation that marks scholasticism.

Anthony's teaching and preaching were so effective that a bishop commissioned him to write sermon notes so that other clerics might preach from them. Anthony took the Mass readings from the lectionary for each Sunday and discoursed on them in his sermon notes. Because he was convinced of the internal unity of the Scriptures, Anthony found what he called concordances between the Hebrew Scriptures and Christian Testament readings and the psalms for each Sunday of the year. His notes tie the readings around one or more main themes, which are supported by secondary themes and a wealth of material. Anthony intended the notes to be a comprehensive collection of preachable material for the clergy for an entire liturgical year.

With his rigorous schedule of preaching, counseling, hearing confessions, teaching, writing, and visiting friars, Anthony had to squeeze in time for prayer. He did this by retreating periodically to hermitages and by his long nightly prayers when everyone else was asleep.

Anthony's faith, preaching, and example resulted in numerous conversions. The hagiographers tell of these in one example after another.

In Rimini, one of the heretic strongholds, Anthony, speaking from a riverbank, preached to the fish when the crowd dispersed. The fish rose to the surface of the water to listen to Anthony. As word of this miracle spread through the town, the incredulous crowd returned not only to hear the preacher but also to accept the faith.

Another time, the story goes, heretics invited Anthony to a banquet. When he realized that the food was poisoned, Anthony asked them why they were trying to kill him. They told him that they were trying to test the validity of Mark's Gospel, which states that believers will be unharmed "if they drink any deadly thing" (Mark 16:18). If Anthony was unharmed, they would join the Catholic faith. Accepting the challenge, Anthony made the sign of the cross over the food and ate it. When he suffered no ill effects, the heretics converted.

Anthony's preaching, however, had its greatest effect among those already in the church. He preached in one town after another, his fame preceding him. When churches became too small to hold the crowds that came, he preached from marketplaces, town squares, and meadows. By the end of his life, he was preaching to crowds of thirty thousand people.

As provincial of Romagna, an area in northern Italy, Anthony visited the beautiful city of Padua. A city of superb architecture surrounded by rolling hills of natural loveliness, Padua seemed to Anthony the most gorgeous spot in the world. The people impressed him as well. He made Padua his home, and its populace embraced the friar as their own son. Thus, in 1230, when a physically weakened Anthony asked to be released from his duties as provincial and was granted his request, he retired to Padua.

Entry into Glory

Anthony suffered from dropsy, a common medieval affliction that is today known as edema. The water retention associated with this illness bloated Anthony so that he appeared corpulent, even though he ate little and frequently fasted.

Even though Anthony was no longer the provincial, he could not retire from his calling. For the last year of his life, he worked to convert Padua and to finish writing his commissioned sermons. In 1231, Anthony preached daily during the entire forty days of Lent and heard confessions until sunset. Immense crowds flocked to hear the friar whom all proclaimed to be a saint.

Priests from Padua and surrounding towns were called in to hear confessions. Repentant sinners would approach Anthony, throwing ill-gotten goods at his feet. Prostitutes would come wailing before him. Heretics, usurers, and wife beaters would publicly confess and receive absolution. At Anthony's insistence, the town law regarding debtors was rewritten, giving indigent people more compassionate treatment.

Following Lent, Anthony continued to preach until Pentecost in late May. Then he retired to Camposampiero, a small friary about ten miles from Padua. In a house built for him in a tree, he continued to write his sermons and pray. Even here he was not left in peace. Crowds came to hear him preach to them. Individuals came for counsel.

After being at Camposampiero for about two weeks, Anthony collapsed at the daily meal. Realizing that death was near, he asked to be taken to Saint Mary's Friary in Padua. But as the rude oxcart that carried the dying man approached the city, it was met by another friar who urged the driver to take Anthony to the nearby convent of Arcella, where he could die in peace. Here Anthony died. The children of Padua began running through the streets crying, "The saint is dead. Father Anthony is dead."

After a bitter struggle over where to bury Anthony's remains, the matter was settled in favor of Saint Mary's. Pilgrims came to the tomb, and immediately miracles began to happen there. Within a year, Anthony was canonized.

Key Elements of Anthony's Spirituality

People considered Anthony a saint because he modeled the virtues that characterized Christ. Even so, like each person, Anthony manifested unique gifts and a spirituality formed with these gifts. Here are some of the important elements of Anthony's spirituality:

The Humanity of Christ

As a follower of Francis of Assisi, Anthony was devoted above all to the incarnate Christ. To refute the Catharist heresy that Christ only *seemed* to be human, Anthony emphasized that Jesus *was* flesh and blood. He drew out beautiful sermons in which he described the Passion in detail or in which he portrayed the helplessness of the newborn Savior. For Anthony, Christ was eternally alive and always present. People can adore him as readily now as at the crib in Bethlehem.

Spreading the Good News

In his day, Anthony was known not as a miracle worker but as a preacher. His spirituality shaped his preaching, but preaching also deepened his spirituality. Anthony believed that all Christians must spread the Good News.

Awareness of Personal Sin

Today we might be aghast at hearing a preacher forthrightly condemn sins that we read about in the newspaper. Anthony spoke forcefully against sin. Because corruption was so evident in both the established church and in society, Anthony confronted it openly.

Anthony, however, never singled out a particular sinner in a sermon. The closest that he ever came to naming one was when he was speaking to a gathering of over a hundred mitered clergy as well as numerous laity in Bourges, France. During his sermon, Anthony turned to the clerics and called out, "You there in the miter," and then began to call forth the sins of the clerics. Afterward, Archbishop Simon de Sully came to Anthony in tears. Anthony never called out the arch-bishop's name, and Simon de Sully was only one of many wearing miters that day.

Anthony knew full well that until people own up to their personal sinfulness, they will not reach out for the loving embrace of God, and their sinfulness will continue to infect their life and the whole community.

Personal Repentance

The main purpose of preaching, Anthony wrote, was to bring the sinner to repentance. Anthony declared that the words of the preacher must go in deep, like a goad. Anthony's sermons focused on making the sinner aware of the gravity of sin and calling the sinner to repentance and to the boundless mercy and love of a forgiving God. Francis wanted all his preaching brothers to emphasize these themes, but Anthony gave them a special focus because he stood in the forefront of those who encouraged frequent and private confession.

Confession

Anthony was a champion of frequent, private confession in an age when most people confessed their sins once during their lifetime and did it publicly. The appeal of being able to go to a priest in private to seek God's forgiveness and reconciliation with the community may be lost today because this practice is taken for granted. But imagine standing before the entire church to confess that you had cheated on your taxes or committed adultery before you could be given a public penance. Then imagine Anthony encouraging you to go to confession privately and receive absolution for the same sins. Most people would opt for private confession. Thus, Anthony's call to conversion and repentance through private confession was embraced by his listeners.

Christian Virtues

From his emphasis on recognition of personal sin and repentance, Anthony naturally came to emphasize the Christian virtues: justice, mercy, poverty, obedience, joy, and humility. Anthony wove his instructions about virtue throughout his sermons like threads of precious gold. In each of his sermons, in a variety of ways, listeners would find themselves convicted of sin, moved to repentance, and then told how to live a holy life.

Anthony for Today

After Mary, Anthony of Padua is arguably the most popular saint. Besides being the finder of lost objects, Anthony and the legends connected with him have inspired many devotions. Portugal, Italy, France, and Spain consider him the patron of seafarers. People in the Basque region of Spain call Anthony the Holy Matchmaker. Basque girls pray for good husbands at Anthony's shrine in Durango. Some admirers of Anthony write S.A.G.—Saint Anthony Guide—on their outgoing mail because he is believed to be the guardian of the mail. Because of his legendary charity, Saint Anthony's Bread is distributed to poor people on his feast.

The prior of the Augustinians at Coimbra was excommunicated in part because of sexual abuse. The sordid example of this man led Anthony to call priests to reform. Anthony consoled abuse survivors and counseled abusers who were trying to reform. As a result, survivors of sexual abuse and repentant perpetrators are urged to pray to Anthony for help in healing. All of these customs and many others attest to the affection that people have for Anthony. His influence lives in the hearts of people now, just as it has for generations.

This is so because people are spiritually hungry today. Indeed, saying this has become a truism. But people in Anthony's time ached for hope, justice, love, and belief too. Through his preaching, consoling, teaching, and celebrating, Anthony drew people to a God who is the one source of all holiness and happiness. Anthony wrote:

> Who can be more blessed or happier than the one in whom God has set up his dwelling place? What else can you need or what else can possibly make you richer? You

have everything when you have within you the One who made all things, the only One who can satisfy the longings of your spirit, without whom whatever exists is as nothing. (Livio Poloniato, ed., *St. Anthony of Padua: Seek First His Kingdom*, p. 11)

Anthony finds lost objects, but more important, he is the saint who finds lost souls. Anthony's example and words can urge us to personal change and to find the Way, the Truth, and the Life. The Way is that of personal conversion to Christ, the Truth is that of God's mercy, and the Life is that of Christ's boundless love.

✧ Meditation 1 ✧

O Infinite Love!
O Incomprehensible
Compassion!

Theme: Fully divine and fully human, Jesus Christ has shown God's love for us by his Incarnation, life, death, and Resurrection. Out of infinite love, he conquered death and shows us the way to life.

Opening prayer: Gracious God, you sent us Jesus to be God-with-us. Your love for us is everlasting. I give thanks now, and may my heart always be filled with gratitude for the gift of yourself.

About Anthony

In his sermon notes, Anthony frequently wrote about the supreme love of God in sending us Christ, God's word made flesh. Anthony was preaching about God's love during a chapter meeting in Arles in 1224. So tenderly did he speak, that Francis of Assisi appeared in a vision to bless Anthony and all those present. Here is how an early biographer described the incident:

Among the brothers was one, a priest of great renown but of more splendid life, Monaldo by name; his virtue was grounded in humility, aided by frequent prayer, and preserved by the shield of patience. Brother Anthony was also present at this chapter, he whose mind the Lord opened that he might understand the Scriptures and speak among all people words about Jesus that were sweeter than syrup or honey from the comb. While he was preaching very fervently and devoutly to the brothers on this topic, *"Jesus of Nazareth, King of the Jews,"* the aforementioned Brother Monaldo looked toward the door of the house in which there were many other brothers gathered and he saw there with his bodily eyes Blessed Francis raised up into the air, his arms extended as though upon a cross, and blessing the brothers. And they all were seen to be filled *with the consolation of the Holy Spirit,* and, from the joy of salvation they felt, what they were told concerning the vision and the presence of their most glorious father seemed entirely believable. (Thomas of Celano, "The First Life of Saint Francis," chapter 18, section 48, pp. 269–270)

Pause: Ask yourself, How much do I love Jesus Christ?

Anthony's Words

Christ's love for us so bound him to us, that it motivated him to descend down to our own wretchedness, as if he could not have lived in heaven without us. . . .

. . . In chapter eighteen of the second book of Kings we read that David, in his grief over the death of Absalom, went up to the room high over the gate and wept mournfully saying: "My son, Absalom, Absalom, my son, would to God that I might die for you!" (18:33). Christ, mourning the death of the human race, like David, ascended the height of the cross and cried there, as attested by St. Paul in his Letter to the Hebrews; "He offered up prayers with a strong cry and with tears" (5:7). Paraphrasing David, Christ could very well cry out: "My son,

Adam, Adam, my son, would that I could die for you,"
that is, "would that my death be helpful to you!" (Poloniato, ed., *Seek First His Kingdom*, pp. 32–34)

Reflection

Anthony always portrayed Christ as making the ultimate sacrifice out of love to redeem us. Jesus Christ became incarnate,
flesh and blood. He "did not regard equality with God as
something to be exploited" (Philippians 2:6), but assumed human poverty, earthly sorrow, the reproaches of sinful human
beings, and a brutal death. His life of supreme love showed
God's great love for us.

Anthony compared Christ with King David, who loved
his rebellious son Absalom with a consuming love that was
not returned. Instead of serving his father in obedience and
honor, Absalom revolted against him. Through lies and treach-
ery, he attempted to seize his father's kingdom for himself.
When David sent his men to stop this takeover, he made it
plain to his officers that he wanted Absalom brought home unharmed. However, one of his generals, fully understanding the
young man's deceit and craving for power, disobeyed David's
orders and murdered Absalom. David was so distraught over
the death of his son that he cried out in anguish, "Absalom,
Absalom, my son, would to God that I might die for you!"

Anthony understood that God's love for us is infinite, far
exceeding even David's love for Absalom. God's anguish over
our alienation led the Creator to be with us in the flesh, to re-
new the sacred covenant with humanity, and to show us once
again how to love one another.

✧ Pray Anthony's words repeatedly, slowly and meditatively: "Christ's love . . . bound him to us." Let the import of
these words and their truth touch your heart and mind.

✧ In order to ponder God's great love for humanity, this
guided meditation on David and Absalom may help. Find a
quiet place where you will not be interrupted. Get comfortable. Close your eyes. Relax.

Imagine yourself as David. You were raised lovingly and had been a shepherd. You grew up in the fields and took good care of your family's sheep. . . .

Through God's wisdom and grace, you become king. Yet you know that you are only a peasant in a king's palace. . . . You love your children. Imagine playing with them, singing to them the songs you wrote to accompany yourself on a harp. Here is your son Absalom, a busy boy with a will of his own. You laugh at his antics, for he seems much like you. . . .

The years pass. Absalom is grown into one of the best-looking young men in Israel. . . . People bask in his good nature and authority. You are certain that he loves you just as deeply. . . .

Then you hear rumors. Absalom is plotting rebellion. . . . These tales cannot be true. Absalom would never turn against you. One day news arrives: Absalom has mustered an army and declared himself king. A welter of feelings hits you. . . .

Your generals advise you to regain control. You concede. But when you think of Absalom, you tell them, "Do not harm my son." . . . You wait, pondering in your heart your child, Absalom. . . .

A courier enters the room. Grave-faced, he marches to you. "Is Absalom safe?" you ask. "Absalom is dead." Again a tide of feelings envelops you. . . . Your beloved son is dead. . . .

A general chides you. "Who can understand this grief? Would you rather the nation die than your son who rebelled against you?"

"Oh, if only I could die for Absalom!" you cry. "If only I could die for him!"

Now ponder this question: If a parent like David could love a child like Absalom this much, how great must God's love for us be?

✧   Although it is true that Jesus took on all the suffering and powerlessness of human beings, his Incarnation also means that he ennobles, dignifies, and exalts human life. The sin of Adam and Eve was that they did not believe that God had

already made them in God's divine image. They partook of
the forbidden fruit because they wanted to be like God; in fact,
they already were. Jesus reminds us once again that we are
made in God's image. Ponder this question: Do I treat myself
as someone who believes that she or he is filled with God's
love and made in God's image? Do I treat others this way?

✧   Talk with God about ways of reminding people that God
loves them. How can you remind your family, friends, and
coworkers, as well as strangers, of God's love for them? Pray
for the grace to turn intention into deed.

✧   How can your family, congregation, or community show
God's love to its members? To others outside the membership?
Work with others in the group to spread God's love from your
family or congregation to your local community.

✧   During the day, perhaps on the hour, pray these words
adapted from the Gospel of John: "God loves the world."

God's Word

Yes, God loved the world so much
that God gave God's only Son,
so that all people who believe in God
may not be lost
but may have eternal life.

(Adapted from John 3:16)

Closing prayer: Pray Anthony's prayer:

O infinite love! O incomprehensible compassion!
To . . . fly down from heaven . . . ,
to assume a human body,
to undergo the infamy of the cross,
to pour out his own blood
to bring back to life his dead children!

(Poloniato, ed., *Seek First His Kingdom*, p. 33)

✧ **Meditation 2** ✧

Bind Us with Love

Theme: God, who created us out of love, loves us fully. In turn, we are called to love God fully and to love other human beings as we love ourselves.

Opening prayer: God, your name is Love. Teach me to love my sisters and brothers.

About Anthony

For Anthony, to separate love of God from love of other people was as impossible as separating blood from flesh. Anthony's love was most evident in the many counsels that he gave his penitents. He was readily available to them, and they trusted his kindness.

Today, Anthony's love of others is most evident in the popular devotion that has made him the patron saint of lost articles. For generations, people have approached Anthony with their frantic requests because they know that he will listen and respond lovingly. Nearly everyone who has ever called on Anthony to find a lost item has a story to tell of something seemingly gone forever that turns up in an odd way.

An incident in Anthony's life is the basis of this devotion. More important, it illustrates that Anthony, like the father of the prodigal son, is filled with forgiving love:

The reason for invoking St. Anthony's help in finding lost or stolen things is traced back to an incident in his own life. As the story goes, Anthony had a book of psalms that was very important to him. Besides the value of any book before the invention of printing, the psalter had the notes and comments he had made to use in teaching students in his Franciscan Order.

A novice who had already grown tired of living religious life decided to depart the community. Besides going AWOL he also took Anthony's psalter! Upon realising his psalter was missing, Anthony prayed that it would be found or returned to him. And after his prayer the thieving novice was moved to return the psalter to Anthony and return to the Order which accepted him back. Legend has embroidered this story a bit. It has the novice stopped in his flight by a horrible devil brandishing an axe and threatening to trample him underfoot if he did not immediately return the book. Obviously a devil would hardly command anyone to do something good. But the core of the story would seem to be true. And the stolen book is said to be preserved in the Franciscan friary in Bologna. (Lothar Hardick, *Anthony of Padua: Proclaimer of the Gospel*, insert)

Pause: Today we associate Anthony's charity with his helping us to find lost articles. Ask yourself, In what particular way do I show charity for my sisters and brothers?

Anthony's Words

Bread, usually served at every meal, symbolizes love. Every good deed ought to be done out of love, as the Apostle Paul writes: "Let all things be done in charity" (1 Corinthians 16:14). A meal would not be complete without bread. The same holds true for love: all other virtues are incomplete without it since love perfects all of them. In Leviticus we read: "You shall eat your bread to the full, and dwell in your land without fear" (26:5). The Lord promises two things: the fullness of love in the soul and peace "in your land," that is, in the heart. Every Christian ought to beg our heavenly Father for this bread, so that with the help of his Son, he may love God above all things, and his neighbor as himself. Let us pray: "Give us this day our daily bread" (Luke 11:13). ("God's Love for His Child," *Saint Anthony Messenger*, May 1986, p. 4)

Reflection

Christian tradition describes love as one of the three theological virtues, that is, a virtue that is a gift from God and draws us to God. The moral virtues like justice and prudence help us love more fully. But love itself cannot be willed or worked on. It is a pure gift, given by God. Love is lived faith and hope; it is the crown of all the virtues and an intimate participation in God's life.

Trying to define love is almost as impossible as defining God, but we know love when we experience it. The grace of love urges us—heart, mind, and will—to nurture and foster the good of others in whatever ways we can. Love invites us to embrace and affirm ourselves. Love always draws us close to God.

Anthony, as a follower of Francis of Assisi, was as poor as Francis. He gave what he most desired to have for himself, his time. People who wanted Anthony's advice besieged him. Anthony attended anyone who came to him. He preached the Good News. In short, Anthony fostered the good of his sisters and brothers in whatever ways he could.

Each of us is called to love God and our neighbor in any way that we can. Love will be the chief criterion for separating the "sheep" from the "goats" at the last judgment, when Jesus will speak these words: "In truth, when you did these things [acts of love] to any one of the least of your sisters and brothers, you did them to me" (adapted from Matthew 25:34–40).

✧ Charity and familial love are two ways of loving. Both ways of loving do good for those people who cannot take care of themselves for one reason or another: being poor, sick, too young, too old, or too disabled to do so. Examine your experience of giving charity and familial love:

✦ Charity: To whom do I show charity—that is, to whom that needs my help do I do good or give service?

✦ Familial love: In what ways do I exercise love for my own children or for children in the community? For elders or disabled people who cannot manage on their own?

❖ Another way of loving is being a friend. Friends mutually and equally care for one another; they are loyal and supportive of one another and they share a common view of the world. Friends are capable of helping one another achieve what is good. Make a list of your friends. How do you show your love for them? How do they show their love for you? How often do you tell these people that you love them?

❖ Some of us are called to love one person in an exclusive way. The desire two people have for union of their bodies as well as their souls distinguishes the love described in many passages from the Song of Songs. Reflect on your love for your beloved. Talk with God about it and ask how you can love your beloved more fully.

❖ Anthony wrote that all virtues are incomplete without love, for love makes all virtues perfect. What virtues do you need to develop in order to love more fully: justice, moderation, prudence, courage, honesty, or forgiveness? Ask God's grace to nurture the virtues that you need most in order to love wisely and well.

Then relax and pray for several minutes, using these words of Anthony: "Love makes all virtues perfect." Let the words flow through you, listening for any special meaning that they might have for you.

❖ Consider how you can do good for people who need help: homeless citizens in a shelter, battered women, illegal residents, people with AIDS, prisoners, or nursing home residents. Pray for the courage, wisdom, and will to act with love.

✧ Who do you find unlovable or, at best, annoying? Why do you find it difficult to love this person? What can you do to be reconciled? How could you get to know the person better? Pray for the person. Greet the person. Ask God to help you do good for the person, even in small ways.

God's Word

If I have the eloquence of humans or of angels, but speak without love, I am simply a gong booming or a cymbal clashing. If I have the gift of prophecy, understanding all the mysteries there are, knowing everything, and having faith in all its fullness to move mountains, but have no love, then I am nothing at all. If I give away all that I possess, piece by piece, and if I even let them take my body to burn it, but am without love, it will do me no good whatever.

Love is always patient and kind; it is never jealous. Love is never boastful or conceited; it is never rude or selfish; it does not take offense, and it is not resentful. Love takes no pleasure in other people's sins but delights in the truth; it is always ready to excuse, to trust, to hope, and to endure.

Love does not come to an end. (Adapted from 1 Corinthians 13:1–8)

Closing prayer: Pray Anthony's prayer:

Lord Jesus,
bind us to you and to our neighbor with love;
may our hearts not be turned away from you,
may our souls not be deceived,
nor our talents or minds enticed
by the allurements of sin,
so that we may never distance ourselves
from your love.
Thus may we love our neighbor as ourselves
with strength, wisdom and gentleness.
With your help, you who are blessed
throughout all ages. Amen.

(Claude Jarmak, trans., *Praise to You Lord:*
Prayers of St. Anthony, p. 30)

Christ, Our Human Savior

Theme: Christ, although fully God, sanctified our human lives and fleshly bodies by becoming fully human. Thus, he teaches us how to embrace our full humanity.

Opening prayer: Gracious Jesus, you are God become flesh. Help me to appreciate this wondrous mystery.

About Anthony

Anthony lived at a time in which many heresies—distortions of Christianity—were circulating widely. One of the most tenacious heresies was Catharism, also called Albigensianism in France. This heresy stated as one of its basic beliefs that all things of the flesh were evil. Therefore, Christ, being all good, could not have assumed human flesh. His humanity, stated the Cathar belief, was an illusion.

Much of Anthony's preaching refuted Catharism, at least indirectly. Although he did not often engage in public debates with the Cathars, he steadfastly preached the full teaching of the church. In doing so, he constantly emphasized Christ's uniqueness in being both fully divine and fully human.

Anthony's preaching on the humanity of Christ may be the basis of the legend in which the Christ Child appeared to him. Anthony's words had so enfleshed Christ to his audiences that the story flourished that Christ, in the flesh, came to rest in the preacher's arms.

> As the Legenda informs us, Jesus appeared to him in the form of a child, allowed Anthony to embrace him, and touched the Saint on the forehead. According to the Legenda, there was a witness to this event. At this precise moment, Count Tiso was passing by the cell of the Saint. He saw a light shining from the room and entered it. Perhaps he wanted to offer some companionship to his sleepless friend. Was the light perhaps so bright that the Count assumed a fire had broken out and came to be of assistance? In any case, he witnessed the miraculous occurrence. Deeply touched, he fell to his knees. (Lothar Hardick, *He Came to You So That You Might Come to Him: The Life and Teaching of St. Anthony of Padua*, p. 108)

Pause: Ponder Jesus, God-with-us, as a baby—vulnerable, dependent, and behaving as all babies do.

Anthony's Words

> In order to help the shepherds find the source of so much joy, the angel gave them a particular sign: "You will find a babe wrapped in swaddling clothes and lying in a manger" (Luke 2:12). Certain characteristics of this sign deserve our attention. What do these words mean if not that you will find Wisdom stammering in simple sounds, omnipotent power in weakness, majesty bent low, the Immense become a babe, the infinitely rich become poor, the King of Angels in a stable, the One whom nothing can contain, lying in a narrow manger. (Poloniato, ed., *Seek First His Kingdom*, pp. 174–175)

Reflection

Anthony was always deeply moved by the contradictions in Christ's divine and human life. Because Christ was fully human, he experienced all the emotions, temptations, and physical needs that humans experience. He is our true savior, but he is truly one of us. To make Christ anything less than fully human, while also fully divine, is to minimize his love for us and the significance of his wondrous life, sacrificial death, and victorious Resurrection.

God took on humanness in order to affirm our human ways of loving. Jesus touched his sick sisters and brothers to heal them. He embraced the children who came to him. He ate fish and bread, and he drank wine with his followers to be in communion with them. He used his arms to work and to overturn the tables of the merchants in the Temple. He was hung to die on the cross because such love as his will always confront the forces of destruction. He became fully God-with-us, Emmanuel, so that we would learn to be God's works of art (adapted from Ephesians 2:10), temples of God (adapted from 1 Corinthians 3:16–17), and images of the loving God (adapted from Genesis 1:26–31). Rather than spurn humanity, Jesus Christ embraced full humanity and showed us its glory and goodness.

✧ Reread Anthony's words and meditate on them. What characteristics do newborn infants possess? Write down words or phrases that describe newborns. Now apply those to Christ. For example, ponder the words, "Christ, you were helpless." Go through your list in this manner. How do you feel about God-with-us, Emmanuel, coming as a baby? How does this picture challenge you? Affirm you? Stir your affection for God?

✧ Jesus fed hungry people and healed those who were sick. He said for us to do likewise. Reflect on these questions:
✦ How can I be, for my sisters and brothers—especially those most in need, Jesus Christ's . . .

> hands?
> voice?
> touch?
> hearing?
> loving presence?

✧ Mary and Joseph protected and nurtured the child Jesus to full maturity. Discuss with God how nurturing your own body, mind, and spirit will assist you in building the Reign of God on earth, and talk with God about any ways that you do not fully appreciate or care for the temple that is your body.

✧ Draw up a list of several statements that affirm your body, for example, "Body and spirit, I am a gift from God," or "I am a wonder of God's creation." Write one or more of these affirmations in fancy lettering and post them in different places around your home. Resolve to pray these affirmations several times a day to remind yourself of God's greatness and of your sacredness as a human being.

God's Word

In the beginning was the Word,
and the Word was with God
and the Word was God.
And the Word became flesh
and lived among us,
and we have seen his glory, . . .
full of grace and truth.

(John 1:1,14)

Closing prayer: Pray Anthony's prayer:

Behold in this child
is found abundance of all good,
our paradise.
Run, then, all you who are hungry
and all you moneylenders,
who prefer money to God,
hurry to buy without money,
without giving anything in exchange,
the grain of wheat which today the Virgin offers you.
She gave birth to a son—
not just any son,
but the very Son of God.

O blessed Mary, you have your Son in common
with God the Father. . . .
She gave birth to her Son.
His Father gave divine nature,
his mother human nature;
his Father gave majesty,
his mother weakness.
In this way, she gave birth to her Son,
to Emmanuel,
to God-with-us.
Who therefore can stand against us.
We should not fear.
Victory is assured to our side
because God is on our side.

(Poloniato, ed., *Seek First His Kingdom*, p. 171)

✧ Meditation 4 ✧

The Passion of Christ

Theme: Christ's Passion, the model of sacrificial love, inspired Anthony's preaching and teaching and his own compassionate life.

Opening prayer: Crucified Savior, with your Passion, death, and Resurrection, you have set us free and shown your love for sinful humans, like me. All glory, praise, and thanks to you, Savior of the world.

About Anthony

Anthony, like all the followers of Francis, frequently emphasized the Passion of Christ in his sermons. Jesus so loved humanity that he healed illnesses, forgave sins, challenged hypocrisy and injustice, and finally gave his life for all women and men. After decades of Franciscan preaching on the real suffering of Christ, crucifixes began to show Jesus beaten and bloody.

Because Anthony meditated so deeply on the suffering, sacrificial Christ, he had a special love for suffering humanity. His compassion showed in the miracles of healing that are recorded in his biographies. For Anthony, the sign of the cross was a sign of compassion. One of his earliest biographers told this story:

A certain inhabitant of Padua, called Peter, had a daughter whose name was Padovana. Although she was four years old, she was absolutely incapable of using her feet and moved like a reptile, crawling with the help of her hands. Furthermore, it was said that, since she suffered from epilepsy, she would often fall and roll around. When Saint Anthony was still alive, her father, as he carried her in his arms while walking through the city one day, met the saint and began to beg him to make the sign of the cross over his daughter. The saintly father, admiring the man's faith, blessed her and sent her away. When the girl's father returned home, he made his daughter stand up on her feet. Supported by a footstool, she immediately began to walk about. Then, having taken away the footstool, her father gave her a cane. Indeed, walking about in the house, the girl always improved. At last, through the merits of most blessed Anthony, she healed completely and did not need any prop whatsoever. And, from that moment when she was blessed, she no longer suffered any illness or even the least falling sickness. (Bernard Przewozny, trans., *Life of St. Anthony: "Assidua,"* pp. 55–56)

Pause: Ask yourself, Does my devotion to the crucified Christ translate into compassion toward others?

Anthony's Words

"Blessed are they who hunger and thirst for justice, they shall have their fill." "My God, my God, why have you forsaken me?" (Matthew 5:6; 27:46).

Those who hunger and thirst for justice render to each person his proper due. In fulfillment of the law, they love God and their brothers and sisters, and in justice they grieve about the sins they have committed. Notice that Christ cried out the words "My God" twice, as if to indicate the twofold love of God and man; the words "forsaken me" emphasise our need for repentance. The Son says to the Father: "Why have you exposed me to so much suffering?"

The Lord speaks of this threefold obligation to justice through the mouth of the prophet Habakkuk: "The just man, because of his faith, shall live" (2:4). A man "just" to himself, has "faith" in God, and has an obligation to "live" with his neighbor. A just man lives with faith in God, loving his neighbor, and judging and condemning only himself. "The man who does not love," says St. John, "is among the living dead" (3:14).

"Blessed are they who show mercy, mercy shall be theirs." "I am thirsty" (Matthew 5:7; John 19:28).

God will be merciful to us if we are merciful to each other. "Parched with thirst, Christ cried out on the cross for mercy but they did not offer him a cup of cool water. Instead they gave a drink of vinegar mixed with gall, which he refused to drink" (Matthew 27:34). Christ did not drink the vinegar and gall, symbols of our sins, as if to indicate his own sinlessness.

The Lord complains about man's lack of mercy through the mouth of the prophet Isaiah: "When I looked for the crop of grapes, why did it bring forth wild grapes?" "I looked for judgment, but see, bloodshed! for justice, but hark the outcry! (5:4,7). The wild grapes, bloodshed and outcry are our sins of greed and licentiousness. (Poloniato, ed., *Seek First His Kingdom*, pp. 60–61)

Reflection

As Anthony meditated on the Passion of Jesus, he empathized with the physical, spiritual, and emotional wounds of his suffering Savior. Although the physical suffering was severe enough, the emotional pain of abandonment, ridicule, and misunderstanding tormented Jesus as well. Jesus is not just a human being who died once and now lives in heaven. He suffers with each suffering person in the world today.

To Anthony, a faithless and sinful world continued to hurt itself and to crucify Christ. God's grief over the sins of the world was ongoing, so much so that Anthony once wrote:

It is truly frightful that the God who once regretted having created us will one day feel sorry for having redeemed us. If after working all year long in his vineyard
a farmer is disappointed because he cannot find ripe
grapes, how much more bitter will be God's disappointment at our fruitlessness? (Poloniato, ed., *Seek First His
Kingdom*, p. 147)

The suffering of the loving Jesus should inspire us to mercy,
justice, and compassion. Thus, the suffering of Jesus will continue to bear fruit in a hurting, wounded world.

✧ In the meditation quoted in the "Anthony's Words" section, Anthony wrote: "Those who hunger and thirst for justice
render to each person his proper due. In fulfillment of the law,
they love God and their brothers and sisters, and in justice
they grieve about the sins they have committed." Make an examination of conscience, using these questions:
+ Do I hunger and thirst for justice?
+ In my relationships, do I give each person her or his due?
+ How do I show mercy to my sisters and brothers?
+ Have I properly grieved over sins that I have committed?

✧ When have you suffered some measure of the Passion of
Jesus? Write about your time of trial in your journal. Did anyone offer help and compassion to you at the time? Did you experience a resurrection of sorts following the pain? If so,
describe it and thank God for it. If not, pray now for God's
grace to help resolve the situation.

✧ Read the Passion of Christ as recorded by one of the
Evangelists. Then, in your imagination, take the role of an
apostle, a Pharisee, and a bystander. Actually, inside ourselves
we sometimes are ardent apostles, Pharisees, and more or less
neutral bystanders. When you ponder Christ's Passion, what
is your apostle part feeling and thinking? Your Pharisee part?
Your bystander part?
Now reflect on someone you know who is suffering—
physically, emotionally, or spiritually. What is the reaction of
the apostle inside you? The Pharisee? The bystander? Which

reactions are strongest and guide your actions toward this suffering person?

Find a way to exercise your compassion for this person.

✧ Take a walk. Find objects that remind you of the Passion, and touch them. For example, touching thorns may help you remember the crown on Christ's head, or you may stroke a reed that is reminiscent of the one that struck his face. Grasp a rough stone and picture Christ falling headlong onto pavement, the heavy cross bouncing against his collapsed body. Gaze up into a sturdy tree and imagine Christ nailed to it. How do you think Christ felt about having the objects of nature, which he created, become the instruments of his torture?

And on your walk, notice signs of how Christ, present in other people, continues to suffer. For instance, consider someone who is ill, shut-in, or disabled, and for whom objects of support have become obstacles. Stairs may be too difficult to climb, medication bottles too tightly sealed to open, stoves and ovens too dangerous to use, and automobiles too risky to drive. Ponder their suffering. What can you do to help them?

God's Word

My God, my God, why have you deserted me?
Far from my prayer, from the words I cry?
All who see me jeer at me;
they toss their heads and sneer:
"You relied on Yahweh, let Yahweh save you!"

. . . .

Do not stand aside: trouble is near
and I have no one to help me!

(Psalm 22:1,7–8,11)

Closing prayer: Pray Anthony's prayer:

By imitating the example of compassion
given us by cranes,
let us soar, high in flight,
so that we do not lose sight
of the land of our destination,
showing the way to those
who may not know the route.
Let us reprove and encourage
those who might grow indolent and halfhearted
on the way.
Let us take turns
at working and resting,
since we cannot persevere
without rest.
Let us carry on our shoulders
anyone who might be weary or tired
from the journey.
During the night watches,
let us be alert in prayer and meditation
by clutching with our minds and hearts
onto Our Lord's poverty and humility
and onto the bitterness of his passion.
Let us warn others
whenever any danger of sin approaches them.
Finally, let us keep away
from the blind vanity of this world,
just as cranes keep away from bats.
(Poloniato, ed., Seek First His Kingdom, pp. 135–136)

✧ Meditation 5 ✧

Cleansed by Compassion

Theme: God is a God of mercy and urges us through Christ's example and divine grace to extend divine mercy to our neighbor.

Opening prayer: Jesus, you showed mercy to the repentant sinner, to the poor, and to the sorrowful. Create a compassionate heart in me.

About Anthony

Today we think of Anthony as a miracle worker, but in his own day he was known primarily as a great evangelist and a man of abundant mercy. Anthony's biographies, some of which are embellished by popular traditions, list one instance of compassion after another—Anthony healing the sick, Anthony raising the dead, Anthony counseling the afflicted, Anthony interceding for abused wives, Anthony pleading clemency for the destitute, and Anthony petitioning for the release of prisoners of war. In all these cases, Anthony feels the pain of those who are suffering and seeks to relieve it.

Many of the stories and legends, like these two from Anthony's hagiography, indicate that almost any inconvenience to another person called forth Anthony's compassion:

At Brive, where he had founded a convent, [Anthony] preserved from the rain the maidservant of a benefactor who was bringing some vegetables to the brethren for their meager repast. . . .

While passing through Provence, France, in 1226, on his way to Italy [to attend a chapter meeting following the death of Francis of Assisi], fatigued from his long journey, Anthony and his companions entered the house of a poor woman, who offered them bread and wine. Unfortunately, in drawing off the wine, the good woman forgot to shut off the tap of the wine barrel. To add to the confusion, already embarrassing to all concerned, a companion of the saint broke the only goblet. Sensing the discomfiture of the poor woman and of his companion, Anthony began to pray. Suddenly not only was the wine glass made whole, but the barrel, also, was filled anew with wine. (Raphael M. Huber, *St. Anthony of Padua: Doctor of the Church Universal*, p. 59)

Pause: When have you encountered an embarrassing situation? Did anyone put you at ease? Thank God now for that person.

Anthony's Words

In the gospel story about the unforgiving servant, we read that after the master had forgiven him a debt of ten thousand talents, "the official went out and met a fellow servant who owed him one hundred denarii. He seized him and throttled him. 'Pay back what you owe,' he demanded" (Matthew 18:28).

The wicked servant in this story, forgetting the compassion extended to him by his master, refused to show mercy to his fellow servant.

As great as is the difference between the ten thousand talents owed by the servant to his master and the one hundred denarii owed to him by his fellow servant, it is still not as great as the difference between a sin committed against God and a sin which our neighbor might commit against us. If God, the Lord of all creation, forgives us to such a degree, should we not forgive our neighbor's mere trifles? Those who do not recall the kindness shown toward them will never be able to extend compassion to others.

Compassion toward our neighbor ought to be threefold: if he sins against us, we ought to forgive him: "Many sins are cleansed by faith and compassion" (Proverbs: 15:27). If he strays from the path of rectitude and truth, we should instruct him: "The person who brings a sinner back from his way will save his soul from death and cancel a multitude of sins" (James 5:20). If he is in need, we must help him: "Happy is he who has regard for the lowly and the poor" (Psalms 40:2). In this way, we will be "compassionate as our Father is compassionate." (Poloniato, ed., *Seek First His Kingdom*, pp. 133–134)

Reflection

Extending compassion to others is fundamental to sanctity. Whether or not the stories about Anthony's compassion are historically accurate, they reflect the general manner of his life. Anthony recognized that we can and ought to show mercy because God shows us mercy first. He also understood that no matter what anyone has done for us, we can never treat anyone as kindly as God treats us.

Often when we think of mercy, we focus on its fruits in the person who is the recipient of the compassion. But mercy has a cost. Anthony was an extremely busy man. He was a leader in his order, holding at various times the offices of custodian, teacher of theology, and provincial minister. Even if he had not preached, the duties of these offices would have kept him constantly on the go. As if these activities were not enough, Anthony had been commissioned by a bishop to write sermon notes for the instruction of the clergy.

Yet, because of Anthony's faith and popularity, he was besieged with people. Toward the end of his life, he had to be assisted by someone to keep from being mobbed on his way to and from his pulpit. Despite this, he continued to show compassion to all who came to him, taking time to listen to their needs and to offer his help. Perhaps his unrelenting selfless-ness contributed to the weakening of his body and his early death. Compassion can take a toll.

On the other hand, as Anthony declared, we are all "cleansed by faith and compassion" of sins, especially selfish-ness. And the cleansing compassion can be shown through forgiveness, instruction, and help.

✧ Often we think that we must go out of our homes to show mercy. But who in your immediate family is in need of your time and understanding? How can you show compassion to that person?

✧ It is far easier to show mercy to those who express their gratitude for it. Do you know anyone who is ungrateful and hard-nosed, but also needy? How can you show mercy to that person?

✧ Reread "Anthony's Words." Note that compassion ex-tends beyond meeting a person's physical needs to forgiving offenses and instructing in the truth. How do his words lead you to show compassion to those around you? Who needs your forgiveness? Your instruction? How can you show com-passion—through forgiveness and instruction—toward your-self?

✧ Thank God for God's mercy. Pray a litany of thanks for all the instances when you have received mercy.

✧ The church teaches that the Christian should engage in the spiritual and corporal works of mercy. The spiritual works of mercy are to convert sinners, instruct the ignorant, counsel the wayward, comfort the sorrowing, bear adversity patiently, forgive offenses, and pray for the living and the dead. The cor-poral works of mercy are seven acts of charity directed toward the physical needs of others. They are to feed the hungry, clothe the naked, give drink to the thirsty, shelter the home-less, tend the sick, visit those in prison, and bury the dead.

Which works do you frequently do? Which ones does your church regularly engage in? Which need more attention from you? From your congregation? Ask God to help you in-corporate these works of mercy into your life. Pray that your church may find a way to meet the needs of a wider range of people.

God's Word

Show mercy just as God has shown mercy to you. Do not judge other people, and you will not be the subject of judgment. Do not condemn, and you will not be condemned. Pardon offenders, and you will receive pardon. Give, and gifts will be given to you in full measure, because the amount you receive will be determined by the amount you give. (Adapted from Luke 6:36–38)

Closing prayer: Pray Anthony's prayer:

Let us ask Jesus Christ,
Our Lord,
to fill us with his mercy,
so that we may practice compassion
with ourselves and others,
not judging nor condemning them,
but forgiving those who hurt us
and helping those who are in need.

(Poloniato, ed., *Seek First His Kingdom*, p. 136)

✧ Meditation 6 ✧

The Justice of God's Reign

Theme: To proclaim belief in Christ means to foster the advent of the Reign of God. The Reign of God is, first and foremost, a reign of justice.

Opening prayer: Just God, open my eyes to the injustices that surround me. Give me a courageous spirit to right wrongs in my world.

About Anthony

Anthony's feet were firmly planted on the earth. He knew only too well the injustices that existed. He was swift to speak out against them, but also to wade directly into the fray and begin to bring about justice in whatever way he could.

Biographers list many anecdotes about Anthony and justice. Some of these stretch credulity, such as the story in which Anthony bilocated to his hometown of Lisbon to defend his father who was falsely accused of murder. In this story, Anthony raises to life the dead child who names the murderer, thus removing all suspicion from Anthony's father.

However, many of the stories about Anthony bringing justice ring true. Just a month before he died, Anthony made a long journey to face Ezzelino da Romano and request the release of his prisoners of war. Two months prior to that, Anthony was instrumental in having a law passed in Padua for the just treatment of debtors.

In Padua, the law allowed an interest rate of 25 to 30 percent, but many usurers charged up to 75 percent interest. It takes no stretch of the imagination to see how this rate of interest could quickly overcome individuals with debt. In nearly every one of his sermons, Anthony spoke out against greed and usury. Many of the usurers, including several members of the clergy, were his converts. The reform of the Paduan law was the result of Anthony converting not only individuals, but an entire city.

St. Anthony, during Lent of 1231, did more than preach on this subject (usury); in an old codex of Padua a statute, dated March 15th of that year, reads:

> It was enacted and ordained that no one henceforth should be held in prison for money debts, past, present, or future, if he forfeited his goods. And this applies to both debtors and their bondsmen. . . . This statute has been enacted at the instance of the venerable brother and blessed Anthony, confessor of the Order of Friars Minor.

It is easy to imagine the relief of the debtors when this statute was proclaimed throughout the city. (Mary Purcell, *Saint Anthony and His Times*, pp. 228–229)

Pause: Imagine yourself a debtor who has just heard the reformed statute that Anthony inspired.

Anthony's Words

"Seek first his Kingdom and his righteousness, and all these things will be given you besides" (Matthew 6:33). The Kingdom of God is the highest good and we must therefore seek it. We look for it with faith, hope and charity. The justice of God's Kingdom consists in observing everything Christ taught us. To seek his Kingdom means to realise fully the justice of the Kingdom through good works. Hence, seek his Kingdom above all else. Make it the most important thing in your life. Everything else must be sought in view of this Kingdom; nothing should be asked beyond it. Whatever we ask must serve that end. (Poloniato, ed., *Seek First His Kingdom*, p. 118)

Reflection

For Anthony, righteousness and justice were synonyms. A righteous person followed every admonition of Christ, and therefore could not help being just. Justice stems from treating others as we would wish to be treated ourselves. Christ showed us the way to establish justice, for he himself was just.

Jesus talked more explicitly about justice than love because love is largely promoted by acting justly. Biblical justice means more than simply giving people their due. Both the Hebrew and Christian Scriptures teach us to reform our ways so that deprivation ceases to exist and peace dwells in the land. Saint Augustine said that "justice consists in helping the needy and the poor" (Daniel C. Maguire, *The Moral Core of Judaism and Christianity: Reclaiming the Revolution*, p. 132). Anthony's admonitions about justice follow in the tradition of the Bible and all the great church teachers. Acting justly builds the Reign of God where "the wolf shall live with the lamb, the leopard shall lie down with the kid. . . . They will not hurt or destroy on all my holy mountain; for the earth will be full of the knowledge of the LORD" (Isaiah 11:6–9).

✧ List ten injustices in the modern world. Order them, according to your view, from the most grave injustice to the least. What can you do about any of these? Can your church take a role in helping to correct some of these injustices? In prayer, ask God to show you.

✧ Do you treat anyone unjustly? Look at your own family or coworkers. Do you tend to treat those whom you get along with better than those who rub you the wrong way? How can you show justice to people you dislike?

✧ Imagine that Christ's second coming happens today. What injustices would he attack? What would he say about them? What would he do? Are there any injustices about which we can do nothing?

✧ How is personal righteousness related to justice? Is it possible to be righteous without being just? Meditate on this.

✧ Do you know anyone who is fair-minded and just? Write that person a note of appreciation and encouragement.

✧ Anthony put his righteousness into just action by pushing for a basic reform in the usury laws of Padua. Is there one local ordinance, state law, or federal law that you find particularly unjust and about which you could do something? How could you, with God's grace, help reform this injustice? Do the candidates for public office that you vote for promote justice—"helping the needy and the poor"?

God's Word

A person's behavior may seem perfectly correct in his or her own eyes, but God takes the measure of the heart.
Acting with virtue and justice pleases God more than sacrifice.

(Adapted from Proverbs 21:2–3)

Closing prayer: Pray Anthony's prayer:

O God, source of all good,
help us to do good,
so we can present to you, who are all good,
an offering of our actions
and hope for a just reward.
Borne by the hands of guardian angels,
may our offering ascend to you,
and may your grace descend on us,
that we may at last arrive at your glory
who are blessed throughout all ages. Amen.

(Jarmak, trans., *Praise to You Lord*, p. 10)

✧ **Meditation 7** ✧

This Is Your Mother

Theme: Mary, the mother of Jesus, was Jesus' first and truest disciple. Mary exemplified all the virtues, but especially love and faith.

Opening prayer: Mary, I greet you as the mother of my Savior. Be for me a model of faith amid difficulty, and love amid rejection.

About Anthony

Anthony possessed a great love for Mary, the mother of Jesus. This devotion began as a child because Anthony's own mother, Maria Teresa, passed her own deep love for her patron saint and namesake on to Anthony.

Because of her full cooperation with God's plan of salvation, coupled with her total faith in her Son, Mary became the standard of the faithful Christian. During Anthony's lifetime, chivalry flourished, and Mary became the maiden to whom all Christian knights pledged allegiance. Yet she was far more than a queen whom people venerated from afar. She was portrayed as a merciful mother who loved and guided the children of faith as she had loved and guided her Son.

In the shadow of the cathedral, to which the pious Portuguese came in pilgrimage because it was dedicated to the Mother of God, [Anthony] felt the power of her intercession, and all his life he had recourse to her protection and help in all needs and difficulties. With her assistance he was able to preserve unsullied in soul and body till his glorious death the shining white garment of a child of God. (Sophronius Clasen, *St. Anthony: Doctor of the Church,* p. 7)

The following legend from an early source is a good example of Anthony's reliance on Mary:

The exhausted Anthony one night gave in to the restoring arms of sleep. Suddenly, Satan leapt upon him and attempted to strangle him. Invoking the name of the glorious Virgin, the Saint made the sign of the cross on his forehead and forced the evil one to loosen his grip. Victorious, Anthony opened his eyes to look on his fleeing enemy, and saw that his cell was bathed in light. (Vergilio Gamboso, *St. Anthony of Padua: His Life and Teaching,* p. 140)

Anthony's devotion to Mary lasted to the end of his life. Right before he died, he prayed, "Oh glorious queen, raised above the stars!" (Gamboso, *St. Anthony of Padua,* p. 130).

Pause: Reflect on your own devotion to Mary.

Anthony's Words

For Anthony, Mary served not only as his mother but also as the mother of the church. She is the mother of all believers. In his sermon for the first Sunday after Easter, Anthony wrote:

"Jesus came and stood in their midst." Jesus' proper place is always in the middle: in heaven, in the Virgin's womb, in the crib between the animals, on the gibbet of the cross. . . .

In the Virgin's womb, since as Isaiah says: "Rejoice, and exult, O habitation of Zion, for great in your midst is the Holy One of Israel" (12:6). O blessed Mary, you who are the habitation of Zion, i.e. of the Church, which established for herself a dwelling place of faith in the

Incarnation of your Son, rejoice in your heart, exult in your eloquent words, "My soul proclaims the greatness of the Lord, etc." (Luke 1:46). "For the great one," yet the small and humble one, "the Holy One of Israel," the sanctifier, is "in your midst," that is, in your womb. (George Marcil, ed., *Anthony of Padua: "Sermones" for the Easter Cycle*, p. 95)

Reflection

Anthony loved Mary as a son would, as well as in the way a servant would. When tempted, he frequently prayed to Mary. In many of Anthony's sermons about Christ, Mary plays a prominent role. After all, she knew Jesus during his entire earthly existence, from his conception in her womb to his Ascension.

Anthony's devotion to Mary never descended to mushy adulation. His was a realistic appreciation of a woman who gave her whole being to God and who lived with God in the flesh in poverty and hardship. The rude stable, the tiny house at Nazareth, the dusty roads of the Holy Land, and the unyielding wood of the cross wove the solid fabric of the Virgin's life. Anthony did not romanticize their harsh reality. Instead, he could understand how Mary transformed the reality of her life with Christ into an unfailing fidelity to him. For Anthony, Mary was the world's most powerful model of the true Christian.

✧ Meditate on the fact that Mary knew Jesus during every moment of his earthly existence. How might her insight into him have changed with the passage of time? How do you suppose this affected her relationship with God?

✧ Anthony's favorite hymn was "O Gloriosa Domina!" Pray the words to the hymn once. Then slowly pray them again, lingering over any passage or passages that you find especially moving or challenging. Then pray the hymn again. When you have finished, pray your own response to Mary.

O Glorious Lady
Raised above the stars,
He who created you with foresight
You fed with milk from your holy breast.

What sad Eve took away
You give back through your beloved Son.
So that we poor wretches might ascend the skies,
You become the window of heaven.

You are the door of the High King.
You are the gleaming gate of light.
Oh, redeemed nations,
acclaim life given you through the Virgin.

Glory to you, Oh Lord,
Who were born of the Virgin,
With the Father and Holy Spirit,
Unto endless ages.

(Geoffrey Chase, trans.)

Anthony spontaneously sang this song on his deathbed. Imagine yourself as a friar standing at his side. What solace would this song have given you? What solace do you suppose it gave Anthony?

✧ Find a comfortable position and close your eyes. Prepare to meditate on Mary, using this guided journey. Relax.

Imagine yourself as a small child of five years old. It is Mother's Day. You and your mother have been to church, and you are both dressed in your Sunday clothes. . . .

You and Mother are walking down a country road, Mother's hand grasping yours, guiding, and maintaining intimate contact. . . .

As you round a bend in the road, a lush, green field yellow with dandelions stretches before you. . . . You wriggle out of Mother's grasp and plunge into the knee-deep grass. You pick one dandelion and another and another. . . . You want to pick a whole fistful of dandelions, as many as you can hold, as a gift for your mother. . . .

You pick another dandelion. Another. You reach again and your hand stops in midair. . . . The glassy eyes of a snake stare up at you from a pointy, scaly head. Shrieking, you bolt from the field, the dandelions bobbing, their stems bending as they brush the grass. Mother is running toward you, her arms outstretched. . . .

Your arms are stretched toward Mother when suddenly your shoe snags a jutting rock and you tumble into the dust, the dandelions splaying from your fist into the grime. The rough pebbles dig into your wrist, and you see a red trickle leak out of your palm and turn the dust into ocher mud. . . .

Mother is there, enfolding you in her arms. You are weeping uncontrollably. Mother is wiping your tears with the skirt of her new, white dress. Then she wipes your bloody palm on the pristine white cloth. . . .

After long, long minutes and much consoling, your sobs subside. Then you see the battered dandelions and begin to wail again. But Mother, still holding you, gathers up the blossoms, arranging their floppy, bent stems to all point down and shaking off the dust. She tucks them into the belt on her dress so that they form a bouquet at her side. "They are beautiful," she says, "and so are you." . . .

As she takes your hand again to lead you home, you ponder her words in your heart. . . .

Paul describes those in heaven as a great "cloud of witnesses" (Hebrews 12:1). Generations of Christians have believed that chief among those witnesses who care for us is Mary. Do you see Mary as loving and cherishing your intentions and you? Is Mary, like the mother in the meditation, someone you turn to in times of trouble? End this meditation by thanking God for giving us a mother who can love us unreservedly, even when we make mistakes.

✧ An old custom names 15 August, the Feast of the Assumption, as Mary's Day. On that day, anyone with the name Mary, or some form of it, is congratulated. You can observe the custom in a personal way. Around the Feast of the Assumption, send a note of congratulation and appreciation to someone named after Mary. Or call that person on the phone, do her a favor, or treat her to something special.

✧ The crucified Christ gave Mary to us as our mother through his words to the Apostle John, "This is your mother." Pray these words repeatedly, and meditate on Mary as the mother of every person, including yourself.

✧ Have you recently told your earthly mother and father how much you love them? If not, tell them today, either in person, by phone, or by letter. If either or both of your parents have died, joining the great cloud of witnesses, speak of your love anyway.

If your relationship with a parent is broken, pray now about how it might be repaired. Relationships can be healed, even if your parents are dead. Ask God to show you how to heal the wounds in your family. Consult someone capable and wise for additional guidance.

God's Word

Standing near the cross of Jesus were his mother, and his mother's sister, Mary the wife of Clopas, and Mary Magdalene. When Jesus saw his mother and the disciple whom he loved standing beside her, he said to his mother, 'Woman, here is your son.' Then he said to the disciple, 'Here is your mother.' And from that hour the disciple took her into his own home. (John 19:25–27)

Closing prayer: Pray Anthony's prayer:

We ask you, Our Lady,
you who are called the morning star,
dispel with your light
the thick fog of allurements to evil
which fills our souls.
Like the light of the moon,
replenish our emptiness,
and dissipate the darkness of our sins,
so that we may attain the fullness of eternal life
and the light of never diminishing glory.
With his help, who made you our light,
and although born from you,
gave you life.
To him be honor and glory
from age to age. Amen.

(Jarmak, trans., *Praise to You Lord*, p. 56)

✧ **Meditation 8** ✧

Unless You Change

Theme: God desires us to acknowledge our sins and to return to full communion with our loving Creator.

Opening prayer: Jesus, you came to preach repentance and forgiveness of sins. Help me to face the lack of love in my own life and be sorry enough for it so that with your grace, I can amend my life.

About Anthony

As an evangelist, Anthony's main goal was to bring his listeners to repentance. Repentance, for Anthony, meant recognition of sin, particularly serious sin, sorrow for such actions, and a change of life that involved restitution and self-discipline. All of this would come about if the listener recognized God's tremendous love in sending Christ to suffer and die for each and every person.

Anthony believed that all preachers should preach repentance. He wrote in one of his sermons, "As a pen writes on a sheet of paper, so should preaching inscribe faith and good morals on the hearts of the listeners. Preaching is also compared to a rod, which is solid, straight, and a means of correction." The words of a preacher, Anthony wrote, "ought to prick the heart of a sinner and elicit the blood of tears"

("Preaching as a Pen and a Rod," *Saint Anthony Messenger,* October 1989, p. 4).

Anthony's words were effective because he, himself, engaged in frequent examinations of conscience and remorse for his own sins and shortcomings. Acknowledging that the potential to sin was ever present in his own soul, he kept keen watch on his thoughts and actions. Anthony spent much time in prayer, and some of it was spent in sorrow for his own failings. No matter what others thought of him, Anthony did not perceive himself as perfect, for on his deathbed, he made his final confession.

Despite his awareness of his own faults and those of others, Anthony always displayed great confidence in God's mercy. Thus, in all his sermons, he spoke forcefully against sin but always drew his sermons to the conclusion that for the repentant sinner, Christ's mercy was bubbling forth to cleanse.

> These Lenten sermons became a religious revival not only for Padua but also for the surrounding district, since people came in great numbers to Padua from outlying villages and hamlets. To all, Anthony appeared as the herald of peace: his words achieved remarkable results. Quarrels were patched up, mortal enemies were reconciled, poor debtors were released from prison and given their freedom, restitution was made of ill-gotten goods. Bad women renounced their evil manner of life, thieves and malefactors became honest men once more, and the whole public life of the citizens and the state once more became Christian in character. (Clasen, *St. Anthony,* pp. 77–78)

Pause: Ask yourself, How deeply have I thought about my sins? How truly sorry am I for them?

Anthony's Words

"A child is born to us, a Son is given to us. . . ." (Isaiah 9:6). We read in the Gospel of St. Matthew that "unless you change and become like little children, you will never enter the kingdom of God" (18:3). Thus the converted sinner is like a child: formerly puffed up with an arrogant heart, boastful in his speech, and proud of his possessions, he now feels humble and small. While lying awake at night, recalling his former life of sin, he cries bitterly just as a baby will cry while lying in his cradle. Nor is the converted sinner ashamed to appear naked and poor in the confessional for the sake of Christ, just like a child feels no shame when he is naked. When the converted sinner is hurt he does not reciprocate in kind, but prays for his persecutors and calumniators for a child does not hate anyone nor does he hold any grudges.

The Holy Mother, the Church, severs the converted sinner from his lustful pleasures with the bitterness of penance just as a nursing mother anoints her breast with bitters when she desires that her child stop nursing. So numerous are the similarities between the converted sinner and the small child who neither desires wealth nor seeks approval from the world.

The fact that a sinner is converted and now a child of God should prompt us to break into song, and with joyful heart and exultant voice, proclaim: "A child is born to us." ("A Child Is Born to Us," *Messenger of Saint Anthony*, December 1984, p. 4)

Reflection

Anthony viewed God as loving the converted person like a mother loves her infant. For Anthony, a sincerely repentant person was truly born anew. To God, a repentant person was a new creation, and the future was bright if the sinner only maintained vigilant watch over all his or her actions. Anthony would be the first to proclaim that heaven was peopled not with the never tempted or the persistently perfect, but with repentant sinners.

Some years ago, renowned psychiatrist Karl Menninger wrote a book entitled *Whatever Became of Sin?* In the book, Menninger examines how psychology can, in part, provide people with ways of denying responsibility for their actions by using factors in their upbringing or heredity. He also explores the dire results in human beings and in society when a sense of sin vanishes.

A healthy sense of sinfulness means that we own our responses to decisions that need to be made, to relationships with people, and so on. A Christian judges her or his sinfulness using the law of love: Have I loved God? Have I loved my neighbor as myself? When we fail, we acknowledge our failure, ask for God's and our neighbors' forgiveness, and grasp God's mercy and the grace to reform our ways.

✧ Reread "Anthony's Words." Meditate on them. Then ask yourself these questions:
✦ Am I like a little child before God, or do I deny my weakness?
✦ Am I willing to bare my soul before God, laying all my sins before God? Or do I hide my sins or try to weasel out of my culpability?
✦ Do I pray for my enemies and detractors?
✦ Do I embrace penance and a willingness to take the hard steps to change my life to a more Christ-like way?
✦ Have I ever imagined heaven rejoicing over my conversion?

✧ If you are not in the habit of making an examination of conscience, take a block of time and do so. Anthony recommended meditating on "the seven major sins which must be confessed in their entirety with all the extenuating circumstances: detraction, hypocrisy, impurity, pride, greed and usury, heresy and obduracy" ("The Desert of Sin," *Messenger of Saint Anthony,* July–August 1985, p. 4). Ask God to show you your failings in each of these areas. Turn the list of your sins into a type of litany, praying after each fault, "Forgive me, O God."

✧ Make a list of those people whose faults and sins you constantly notice. Ask God to help you first cast the beam out of your own eye before you go about correcting others.

✧   Pray this phrase slowly and repeatedly, "Lord, be merciful to me, a sinner." Ponder any images, memories, and feelings that arise as you pray.

✧   Think of one person whom you have offended. Pray about your behavior toward that person. Ask God what you can do to make restitution.

✧   How has your community failed in meeting the needs of people, especially needy people? What can you do to help your community live up to its responsibilities?

God's Word

Imagine that you have one hundred sheep. Tell me which one of you would not try to find one lost sheep, even if it meant leaving the rest. Then imagine the gladness when you found it. You would carry it on your shoulders, and when you got home you would gather your friends and neighbors and say, "Help me celebrate finding this lost sheep!"

If we celebrate finding one lost sheep, consider how much more rejoicing there will be in heaven over one sinner who repents than over ninety-nine good, virtuous people who do not need to repent. (Adapted from Luke 15:4–7)

Closing prayer: Pray Anthony's prayer:

My Lord,
I cannot place the treasure of a sinless life
on the scales of your judgment.
Do not impute this debt to me,
O good God.

(Jarmak, trans., *Praise to You Lord*, p. 8)

✧ Meditation 9 ✧

Pour Out Your Heart

Theme: Repentance for sin, if genuine, will be followed by confession.

Opening prayer: Accepting Christ, let me never fear to confess my sins to you and to those who minister in your name, for you have declared that those who are repentant are forgiven.

About Anthony

Anthony lived at a time in which the church's view of penance was changing. Just about the time that Anthony became an Augustinian friar, the Fourth Lateran Council issued two canons that had a great bearing on the ministry of the future evangelist.

Canon 10 stated that the power to preach, which previously had been delegated mainly to bishops, had to be broadened to include other members of the clergy. This meant that priests and other religious could now preach. This canon paved the way for Anthony to be given an evangelistic mission.

Canon 21 bound the faithful to yearly confession of sins to their parish priest. This was a great change, because previously, public confession of sin once or twice in a lifetime was the generally accepted norm.

73

After he was ordained, a main purpose in all of Anthony's preaching was to induce his listeners to repentance followed by confession and then satisfaction for sins. He was remarkably successful in his goals, not only because he preached, but also because he was willing to spend time listening to the many penitents who came to him. For example, during Lent of 1231, Anthony preached every day for the entire forty days and heard confessions until sundown, breaking his fast only when the last sinner hurried home in the evening twilight.

> Anthony's main concern was to bring [people] back to peace with God. Hence, when the sermon was finished, he immediately began to hear confessions. Such a great crowd of the faithful, men and women, besieged the confessionals, that the friars and other priests of the city whom Anthony had called to his assistance, could hardly satisfy the demands made on them. Even with this help, Anthony, who began to hear confessions immediately after his Mass and sermon, often did not leave the confessional until evening. This meant that throughout the Lenten season he had to fast all day until nightfall. Among the penitents there were many who told their Father Confessor that a vision had brought them to his feet: at night in their dreams Anthony had appeared to them and counseled them to regain God's pardon and friendship by a good confession. (Clasen, *St. Anthony*, p. 78)

Pause: Think of the worst sin that you have ever committed. Did you seek reconciliation for this sin? If so, how did you feel afterward? If not, should you seek reconciliation even now?

Anthony's Words

In one of his sermons, St. Bernard says: "Confession cleanses everything." The prophet Jeremiah, in his Lamentations, gives this advice: "Pour out your heart like water in the presence of the Lord" (2:19). Note carefully that we are to pour out our hearts like water, and not like wine, or milk, or honey. After it is poured out, wine leaves behind its odor in the container; milk leaves a residue within the container, and honey leaves its flavor behind. Water, on the other hand, leaves no trace at all behind in the container. The residue of odor of wine left behind in the container symbolizes the image of sin; the color of milk represents the admiration of vain beauty; and the flavor of honey symbolizes a recollection of previous sins with a certain illicit pleasure. These accursed remnants of sin are mentioned in the Psalms: "Their sons are sated," that is, with evil deeds and the filth of sin, "and they bequeath their inheritance to their little ones," that is, to their passions (16:14). You, however, when you pour out your heart in confession, let it flow out like water, thoroughly washing away all the dregs of evil, and thus you will be cleansed of all your sins. ("Six Means of Purifying the Soul," *Messenger of Saint Anthony*, October 1985, p. 4)

Reflection

Let's face it. Many of us are comfortable with telling God that we are sorry for our sins, but extremely uncomfortable with confessing our sins to another person. It seems easier to talk to God in private, without bringing another human being into the picture. And often the human being to whom we would speak is someone who knows us quite well.

Simply going to God alone, without confessing to another person, may lead to forgiveness of our sins, but it is often insufficiently healing for us. Another human being can say to us, in effect, "Well, now that I know all about that sinful aspect of your life, I still love you. I still accept you." When we hear or sense those words from a human being, we are more likely to realize that they echo the words of God.

If we have offended a friend, we may think that we are sorry, and we may be genuinely sorry. But if we say nothing to our friend about our remorse, we do not effect a healing. If we write a letter to our friend, we have gone further, but perhaps not far enough. A letter may be misunderstood. The person may wonder why we did not speak to her or him face-to-face. But if we face the one whom we have hurt and apologize in an effort to repair the friendship, we open the door to a full healing of the broken relationship. Confessing to another person effects this healing of our relationship with God, can be an opportunity for guidance, and can assure us that we are still acceptable to God and to others.

✧ How often do you confess your sins to another? Talk with God about this, asking, "Am I seeking reconciliation often enough? How often do you want me to seek reconciliation?"

✧ Reread "Anthony's Words." Ask yourself, Is anything holding me back from making a full and sincere confession? Ask God to give you the grace to be reconciled completely and freely.

✧ Consider who you could go to for a confession of your sins and reconciliation. Who would be able to listen lovingly, perhaps give good counsel, and pray with you for reconciliation?

About what matters do you most need to be reconciled with the people of God? How have you harmed community and the earth that you share with them? How have you shown disrespect for your sisters and brothers?

God's Word

If we say that we have no sin, we deceive ourselves, and the truth is not in us. If we confess our sins, [God] who is faithful and just will forgive us our sins and cleanse us from all unrighteousness. (1 John 1:8–9)

Closing prayer: Pray Anthony's prayer:

O house of God,
O gate of heaven,
Confession of sins!

Blessed is [the one] who abides in you.
Blessed is [the one] who passed through you.
Blessed is [the one] who has humbled [the] self within
    you.
O, the mercy of God!
O, the excellence of a repentant heart!
[The one] who dwells in eternity
has deigned to come
and live in the humble heart
of a repentant sinner.

                (Jarmak, trans., *Praise to You Lord*, p. 18)

There Is Joy in Poverty

Theme: By voluntarily embracing poverty, Jesus showed us how simplicity and detachment from material possessions can open the door to spiritual wealth.

Opening prayer: Jesus, poverty was the garment of your life. Show me how to become poor for your sake so that I may be rich in your sight.

About Anthony

Anthony voluntarily accepted poverty of the most radical type. As the son of a well-to-do knight in Lisbon, Anthony could have followed his father's life of relative ease. Instead, while still a teen, he gave up his inheritance and career to become an Augustinian priest.

When Anthony met the poor friars of Francis of Assisi, he was drawn to their radical poverty and total dependence on God. So he petitioned to leave the security of the Augustinian convent to possess absolutely nothing. His voluntary embracing of radical poverty was one of the profoundest joys of his life.

Anthony's honesty and commitment to poverty were sometimes challenged. One test, recorded in his hagiography, came from Ezzelino da Romano, a vicious tyrant.

[Ezzelino] began to doubt the rectitude and honesty of the saint, and he resolved to try him in a cunning manner. He sent him a present of great value through his attendants, commanding them to present it to him with great humility and submission, but with this condition: that if he accepted it, to kill him immediately; if he did not accept it, or rejected it with contempt, to leave him alone and not use violence. They went at once to where Anthony was, and, having saluted him with reverence, said, "Father, your son, Ezzelino da Romano, begs you to accept this gift which he sends you as a mark of the esteem he has for you, and asks you to pray to the Lord for him."

Anthony, moved by a holy anger, rejected the gift and reproached them, protesting that he did not wish to receive anything which came by unjust gains and rapines, and ordered them to leave the house at once, so that it might not be contaminated by their presence. These malicious men, confused and terrified, returned to Ezzelino, who, when he heard what had happened, said: "Truly, he is a man of God; leave him in peace, and let him say what he wishes." Ezzelino knew well that the saint did not cease to denounce his cruelty, and for this reason some say he induced himself to try the saint's virtue by means of gifts. (Ubaldus da Rieti, *Life of St. Anthony of Padua*, pp. 90–91)

Pause: How would you have reacted to Ezzelino's gift?

Anthony's Words

Poverty is fittingly symbolized by gold: whoever possesses poverty is rich and wealthy. Where there is real poverty, there is found abundance; where there is plenty, there is always a need for more. St. Bernard notes: "There is lack of nothing in heaven, except of poverty. This breed is found only on earth and people do not realize its true worth. This is why the Son of God came on earth to seek it out and bestow on it its precious worth." Genesis says that "there is gold in the land of Havilah, and the gold of that land is excellent" (2:11–12). The name Havilah means "To give birth" and is an appropriate symbol of the Virgin Mary.

After giving birth to the Son of God, she wrapped him in swaddling cloths of golden poverty. O inestimable worth of poverty! Who does not possess you, possesses nothing, even though he may possess everything. There is joy in poverty; in wealth is found only grief and disappointment. (Poloniato, ed., *Seek First His Kingdom*, p. 82)

Reflection

Anthony took to heart Christ's warning that his followers are unable to serve both money and God. Our concerns about material well-being, life's necessities, and bills coming due often keep us from focusing on the riches of God. Anthony, like Christ, continually preached against greed and its accompanying trust in wealth as opposed to trust in God.

Poverty is not a virtue in itself. Indeed, poverty can often lead to sin when those who have little steal or kill to gain more. But poverty can certainly become a virtue when it is voluntarily sought as a way to simplify and purify one's life. Being aware of what we have and sharing our resources with those who need help is certainly a part of Franciscan, biblical poverty. One of the best descriptions of biblical poverty comes from the Book of Proverbs:

> Give me neither poverty nor riches;
> feed me with the food that I need,
> or I shall be full, and deny you,
> and say, 'Who is the LORD?'
> or I shall be poor, and steal,
> and profane the name of my God.
>
> (30:8–9)

When we live close enough to the limits of our resources, we live with a reminder that we can always rely on God's love for us. When gratification of every whim becomes the norm, we need to ponder the "inestimable worth of poverty" and consider choosing it, in some measure, for ourselves.

✧   Pray these words of Anthony slowly and repeatedly; let their meaning for you become clear. Be open to their challenge: "Where there is real poverty, there is found abundance; where there is plenty, there is always a need for more."

✧   The Bible mentions tithing. Many people give 10 percent of their gross income to God. The tithe comes from the earliest accounts in Genesis where Abram gave Melchizedek, priest of Salem, a tenth of everything (adapted from 14:20), and Jacob vowed to God a tenth of all that God gave to him (adapted from 28:22). Converse with God about tithing if you do not already tithe. Discern if this is one way you can answer the call to biblical poverty. You might give your money to your church or to a worthy charity.

✧   Francis of Assisi said that God is pleased when poverty is voluntary. Examine your own lifestyle in light of Francis's remark and Anthony's plea for poverty. How can you simplify your life's necessities? Can you move toward simpler meals, clothes, and housekeeping? List five first steps toward living more simply, and then pray for God's guidance and power to take the steps.

✧   If you are not presently serving poor people, ask the guidance of the Holy Spirit to understand how you can share your time, talents, resources, or skills with them. Perhaps you could volunteer at a homeless shelter, a soup kitchen, a shelter for battered women, a food bank, or a health center for indigent patients. Have you ever thought of approaching grocery stores, bakeries, and restaurants and asking them to donate to a local soup kitchen or food bank? Consider tutoring adults who do not know how to read and write. Pray about taking on some ministry with God's poor people.

God's Word

A rich young man told Jesus, "I have kept all the commandments. What more do I need to do to have eternal life?"

Jesus answered, "If you desire to be perfect, go, sell all your possessions and distribute the money among poor people. Then you will store treasure in heaven. After that, come and journey with me." Upon hearing these words, the young man walked away sad because he was very wealthy.

Then Jesus warned his disciples, "Listen carefully, rich people will enter heaven with great difficulty. It will be simpler for a camel to pass through the eye of a needle than for rich people to get into heaven."

Shocked by Jesus' words, the disciples asked, "Who can be saved then?"

"For human beings on their own," Jesus replied, "it's impossible. However, everything is possible with God." (Adapted from Matthew 19:16–26)

Closing prayer: Pray Anthony's prayer:

We thank you,
O glorious Virgin,
because through you
God is with us.
You gave birth
to your firstborn Son,
who was begotten by the Father
before the beginning of time,
the firstborn of those
who rise from the dead,
the firstborn
of many brothers and sisters.
O poverty, O humility!
The Lord of all creation and of everyone
is wrapped in poor clothes,
the King of Angels is born in a stable.
Blush for shame, insatiable avarice!
Extinguish yourself, human pride!

(Poloniato, ed., Seek First His Kingdom, p. 172)

✧ Meditation 11 ✧

Humble of Heart

Theme: Jesus, who is the Son of God, lived among common folk and trained as a carpenter. His simplicity and gentle power confronted the proud and arrogant people of his time and ours. Christ's humility admonishes us to keep a proper relationship with God and our fellow human beings.

Opening prayer: Living God, teach me the meaning of true humility through the example of your Son.

About Anthony

Anthony was a brilliant man of many talents. His natural grace and charm lent him a charisma that even his enemies noticed. Through years of meditation on and in-depth study of the Bible, Anthony had, according to legend, memorized both the Old and New Testaments in their entirety. His understanding of the natural sciences, as they were known in his day, and his study of the church fathers, as well as his keen powers of observation, put a wealth of knowledge and insight within his grasp. Moreover, God had gifted Anthony with a voice that an early biographer compared to a trumpet. His personality, knowledge, faith, articulateness, and commanding voice could hold audiences spellbound for hours.

Despite these qualities, Anthony never sought attention or adulation. On the contrary, his greatest wish was to live quietly away from the glare of attention, but he accepted God's working through the ministers in his order. Thus he became the public figure we know.

Anthony's desire to remain unknown manifested itself in this early incident. After Anthony returned from a trip to Morocco, he, as a new friar, attended a chapter meeting of the Franciscan order.

> Once the chapter was concluded as usual, and when the ministers provincial had sent the friars entrusted to them to their destinations, only Anthony remained abandoned in the hands of the minister general, not being requested by anyone of the other ministers, like a man who is considered inexperienced and of little use, and because he was not even known. At last, when he called apart Friar Gratian, who was then governing the friars in Romagna, the servant of God began to entreat him that, once released by the minister general, he be taken to Romagna and there be taught the rudiments of their spiritual life.
>
> He neither mentioned his studies nor boasted of the churchly ministry he had exercised; instead, out of love for Christ, hiding all his knowledge and intelligence, he declared that he wished to know, thirst for, and embrace only Christ, and him crucified.
>
> Friar Gratian, having esteemed his admirable devotion, assented therefore to the wishes of the man of God and, taking him with himself, brought him to Romagna. When Anthony, through God's disposition, reached the place, he devoutly retired, after he had obtained permission, to the hermitage of Monte Paolo, where he entered into the peace of silence. (Przewozny, trans., "*Assidua*," pp. 9–10)

Pause: Ask yourself, How do I view my talents and skills? Solely as products of my own effort? As of little worth? As blessings from the Creator? As a mixture of all these attitudes?

Anthony's Words

The heart is the first organ in the human body to be formed. It is also the centre and seat of the virtue of humility: "Learn from me, for I am gentle and humble of heart" (Matthew 11:29). Humility precedes all other virtues, since it informs them and exerts a great influence on their development, providing an impetus for all good deeds. Humility is rightly called "the mother and font of all virtue." According to Solomon, "a live dog is better than a dead lion" (Ecclesiastes 9:4). This is interpreted to mean that the humble publican in the Gospel is better than the proud pharisee: the more, in fact, the publican humbled himself, the more he was exalted. St. Bernard writes: "The deeper the foundation of humility, the higher will the building arise." Humility is more noble than the other virtues because it bears contempt and dishonesty patiently and humbly. It makes itself evident in the comportment of the body, and primarily in the eyes: "A proud eye betrays a proud heart" (St. Augustine) and Sirach exhorts: "Do not give me proud eyes" (23:5). The publican in the Gospel did not dare "to raise his eyes to heaven. All he did was beat his breast and say, 'O God, be merciful to me, a sinner'" (Luke 18:13). The heart cannot be contented with sorrow or pain. The same is true of real humility: it does not grieve because of injuries inflicted, nor does it be[moan] another's good fortune. And rightly so, for if humility suffers, the fabric of all the other virtues is impaired. This is why St. Gregory says: "Who acquires virtues without practicing humility is like a man who carries dust in a strong wind." (Poloniato, ed., *Seek First His Kingdom*, pp. 156–157)

Reflection

Anthony became an evangelist of great renown. By the end of his life, his audiences numbered thirty thousand, a staggering number considering that he preached without any electronic voice amplification. His fame and holiness were well known, and the general public proclaimed him to be a saint even during his own lifetime.

All the praise heaped upon him could easily have gone to Anthony's head, but it did not. Some biographies state that the pope asked Anthony to come to Rome and work at the Lateran, but he refused. His greatest wish was to write a book of theology for laypeople, a dream that he never realized for he simply ran out of time to do it. Despite his work on sermons that a bishop had commissioned, Anthony always had time for common folk. Even during his final weeks, when he worked on his sermons in a tree house outside of Padua, he would stop work to speak to those who came seeking his guidance. A truly humble man, Anthony patterned himself after Christ who made himself the servant of all.

Fundamentally, having humility—like Anthony's—means that we have no delusions about ourselves. We keep ourselves planted on the ground (*humus* in Latin). We appreciate the gifts that God has blessed us with and own our limitations and sinfulness. Most of all, being humble means that we embrace one essential fact: we are completely dependent on our Creator in whose hands we live, move, and have our being.

✧ Reread Anthony's words on humility and meditate on them. Then listen to what God tells your heart about your own humility.

✧ Do an examen of consciousness about humility. These questions may guide you:
✦ List your skills, talents, and gifts. Then ask yourself: When I think of each of these, do I appreciate and nurture each one as a gift from God? Do I assume that they are solely the fruits of my own effort?
✦ Do I judge that my work is more important and meaningful than most people's work? Or do I think of my work as more insignificant and meaningless?
✦ Do I think that I am more virtuous or more sinful than others in my church?
✦ Do I consider myself smarter or less intelligent, wiser or more naive, or better looking or uglier than others?

✦ What do my answers tell me about my humility? Do I have an appreciation for my blessings and a keen sense of my limitations and dependence on God's goodness?

✧ As a reminder of your reliance on God's grace and power, pray a litany of petitions for help that you need from God: for instance, "For the ability to deal with my mother's forgetfulness and impatience, I ask your help, my God."

✧ As a reminder of the blessings that God has given you, pray another litany, this time giving thanks: for example, "For having a sense of humor, especially my ability to laugh at myself, thank you, good and gracious God."

✧ Do something this week to foster humility. Here are a few suggestions: offer to do a simple task for a neighbor, church, or community agency; volunteer to work behind the scenes for some event; or make an anonymous charitable donation.

✧ Francis of Assisi used to say, in a modern paraphrase, "One is as much as one is in the sight of God, and no more." In the sight of God, who are you? Compose a eulogy for your funeral that God would give if God were the homilist.

✧ Pray daily, "God, help me find a true sense of who I am in your sight."

God's Word

Jesus told this story to a group that took extraordinary pride in their virtues and scorned others: "A Pharisee and a tax collector went to the Temple to pray. The Pharisee stood there and recited this prayer to himself, 'God, I thank you that I am not greedy, unjust, and lustful like the rest of humanity. I am especially glad that I am not remotely like that tax collector over there. Twice each week, I fast. I tithe on all my income.' The tax collector tried to stand in an obscure corner and did not dare to raise his eyes toward heaven. He prayed simply, 'Be merciful to me, O God, I am a sinner.' I tell you, the tax collector re-turned home in harmony with God. The Pharisee did not. Those people who exalt themselves will suffer humilia-tion. Those who are humble will be exalted. (Adapted from Luke 18:9–14)

Closing prayer: Pray Anthony's prayer:

Christ Jesus,
you conquered the pride of the evil one
by the humility of your incarnation:
grant also to us
to shatter the chains of pride and arrogance
by the humility of our heart,
so that we may be worthy of the gift of your glory.
With your help
who are blessed from age to age. Amen.

(Jarmak, trans., *Praise to You Lord*, p. 46)

He Was Obedient to Them

Theme: We are called to model our lives after Christ who conformed to God's will even though it led to death on a cross. So we must obey—from the Latin word for "listen to"—God's will.

Opening prayer: Spirit of God, fill me with a desire to seek and to obey your holy will.

About Anthony

When Anthony entered religious life, he took a vow to obey his brothers. This vow eventually led Anthony into his evangelistic ministry.

> At the end of some time, it happened that friars were to be sent to the city of Forli to receive holy orders. For this reason, when Franciscan and Dominican friars had gathered there from different parts, Anthony was among them.
>
> As the time of the ordination approached and the friars were gathered together as usual, the local minister began to ask the Dominican friars who were present to address an exhortation to those thirsting for the word of salvation. But, when each one began to say quite resolutely that he neither wanted nor ought to preach something

improvised, then the superior turned to Friar Anthony and ordered him to proclaim to those who were assembled whatever the Holy Spirit might suggest to him.

The superior did not believe that Anthony knew any part of the Scriptures nor thought that he had read anything beyond, perhaps, what concerned the Church's Office. He trusted only one indication, that is, he had heard Anthony speak Latin when necessity required it. In truth, although Anthony was so industrious that he relied on his memory rather than on books, and although he abundantly overflowed with the grace of mystical language, the friars nonetheless knew him as more skillful in washing kitchen utensils than in expounding the mysteries of Scripture.

Why say anything else? Anthony resisted as much and as long as he could. At last, because of the loud insistence of all those present, he began to speak with simplicity. But when that writing reed of the Holy Spirit (I am referring to Anthony's tongue) began to speak of many topics prudently, in quite a clear manner and using few words, then the friars, struck by wonder and admiration, listened to the orator attentively and unanimously. Indeed, the unexpected depth of his words increased their astonishment; but, to no lesser degree, the spirit with which he spoke and his fervent charity edified them. Filled with holy consolation, they all respected the virtue of humility, accompanied by the gift of knowledge, that was manifest in the servant of God.

Inasmuch as, according to the Lord's saying, "a city built on a mountain cannot be hidden," shortly thereafter the minister was informed of what happened. Anthony, therefore, broke his peaceful silence and was constrained to turn to the public. When the duty of preaching was imposed on him, the faithful dweller of the hermitage was sent out into the world and his lips, closed for so long, were opened to proclaim the glory of God. (Przewozny, trans., "*Assidua*," pp. 10–12)

Pause: Reflect on Anthony's discomfiture and his obedience despite it.

Anthony's Words

After Mary and Joseph found Jesus in the temple, "he went down with them, and came to Nazareth, and was obedient to them" (Luke 2:51). . . . Let all boasting cease, let all impudence disappear in the face of these words: "he was obedient to them." Who was he, who was obedient? He who has created everything from nothing. He "who," as Isaiah says, "has cupped in his hand the waters of the sea, and marked off the heavens with a span; who has held in a measure the dust of the earth, weighed the mountains in scales and the hills in a balance" (40:12). "Who," as Job says, "shakes the earth out of its place, and the pillars beneath it tremble; who commands the sun, and it rises not; who seals up the stars; who alone stretches out the heavens and treads upon the crests of the sea; who made the Bear and the Orion, the Pleiades and the Constellations of the south; who does great things past finding out, marvellous things beyond reckoning (9:6–10). He who does all these things "was obedient to them." Whom did he obey? A carpenter and a poor, humble virgin. He who is the beginning and the end, the ruler of the angels, made himself obedient to human creatures. The creator of the heavens obeys a carpenter, the God of eternal glory listens to a poor virgin. Has anyone ever witnessed anything comparable to this? Has any ear heard anything like this? Let the philosopher no longer disdain from listening to the common labourer, the wise man to a simple one, the educated to the illiterate, a son of a prince to a peasant." (Poloniato, ed., *Seek First His Kingdom*, pp. 159–160)

Reflection

The Catholic church recognized Anthony's intelligence and faith by naming him a doctor of the church. Despite his intelligence, he was often subject to illiterate superiors. Even Francis of Assisi was not a particularly well-educated man. Yet Anthony obeyed these men without question. For instance, he taught the friars theology only when Francis assigned him to do so. He wrote his famous sermons only when requested by ecclesiastical superiors.

Anthony's preaching took him into the very heart of his world. Most of his listeners were illiterate. A good many were poor. He spoke to all with love and conviction. And Anthony listened to the voice of God no matter who spoke it. He realized that in its broadest terms, God's will is for us to love and to do good. Anthony heard that call from many different sources.

✧   Jesus gives us two commands, to love God and to "love one another; just as I have loved you" (John 13:34), and then leaves most of the particulars up to us. Bring to mind several decisions that you are in the process of making; pick one to spend time discerning with God's Spirit. Here are some guides to your discernment:

+ Explain to the Spirit all the facets of the decision that you are aware of.
+ Recall biblical stories related to your situation or, if necessary, search the Gospels and the Epistles for the advice that Jesus has for you.
+ Talk with the Spirit some more.
+ Discuss the situation with someone you trust and who can help you.
+ After praying for wisdom and power, act, knowing that God will be with you.

✧   Anthony remarked, "Let the philosopher no longer disdain from listening to the common labourer, the wise man to a simple one, the educated to the illiterate, the son of a prince to a peasant." Anthony listened to God's calls to service in his ordinary experiences: people's requests for advice, the superior asking him to speak. Examine your life of the last few days. When have you been asked to give love, to act with justice, or to serve? How did you respond?

✧ If you are in a position of authority over anyone, either at work or in your family, examine your leadership style. How would you describe your exercise of authority? Pray about your style. Ask God to show you how to exercise authority as Jesus did.

✧ On Pentecost, Jesus sent the Holy Spirit to be God's voice within us, guiding and teaching us. Pray daily, "Holy Spirit, let me know your will for my life. Grant me the grace to do your will each moment of this day."

God's Word

Jesus went with Mary and Joseph to Nazareth. He obeyed them. His mother cherished in her heart all that he had done. So Jesus grew steadily in wisdom, in power, and in favor with God and other people. (Adapted from Luke 2:51–52)

Closing prayer: Pray Anthony's prayer:

Lord Jesus Christ,
may we board the boat of Simon Peter
with the virtue of obedience.

. . . .

Help us cast our fishing nets
that we may get a great catch of good works
and attain to you, good and great God,
who reign gloriously through ages. Amen.

(Jarmak, trans., *Praise to You Lord,* p. 28)

Pray for All Your Needs

Theme: We speak to God through prayer and come to know God through contemplation.

Opening prayer: God, you are only a thought away. Give me the joy of continuous communication with you.

About Anthony

Anthony was a man of prayer. He girded his day with the Divine Office and the liturgy of the word. Nights were spent in prayer and meditation. Whenever he could get away from the crowds that besieged him, he would find a secluded spot to pray. Time after time, the biographers mention Anthony's deep prayer life. When his skeleton was exhumed in 1981, his kneecaps showed evidence of bursitis, the likely outcome of hours spent kneeling.

Anthony would have been happy to spend his life in prayer and meditation. As a youth, he asked to leave Saint Vincent's Monastery in Lisbon because he was bothered too much with visits from family and friends. Upon his transfer to Holy Cross Monastery in Coimbra, about a hundred miles distant, Anthony had the uninterrupted prayer time that he craved. As a Franciscan friar assigned to Monte Paolo, Anthony found a secluded grotto in which to pray.

While Anthony was staying in that hermitage, a certain friar built himself a cell in a grotto which was suitable for prayer and where he could dedicate himself more freely to God. When the man of God saw it one day and realized how appropriate it was for growth in devotion, he went to entreat the friar and humbly asked him to cede to him the use of that cell. At last, when he obtained the place of peace, the servant of God, after fulfilling the morning community prayers, would daily retire to the cell, taking with himself some bread and a small container of water. In this way, he spent the day alone, forcing the body to serve the spirit; but, in observance of the holy norms, he always returned on time for the friars' reunion. (Przewozny, trans., "*Assidua,*" p. 10)

Pause: If Anthony asked you to describe your prayer life, how would you describe it to him?

Anthony's Words

The Apostle in his letter to Timothy shows the procedure to be followed in asking and beseeching God, "I urge first of all that supplications, prayers, petitions, and thanksgivings be made" (1 Timothy 2:1). "Supplication is an urgent pleading to God in spiritual exercises. . . . Prayer . . . is the expressly affectionate state of a person united to God, during which state the enlightened soul speaks with God in a familiar and respectful manner and enjoys his presence as long as his grace allows. Petition is any prayerful attempt at obtaining some of life's temporal needs. In petition, while approving the good will of the petitioner, God still does what he judges better; and he gladly gives to one who asks rightly. Consider the following example of a petition taken from the Psalms, 'But despite their wickedness, my prayer is that good things accrue to them' (140:6). Petition, we know, is made also by the wicked, for it is common to all men. But the children of this world in particular long for peace and tranquility, bodily health, good weather, and other such things that have to do with this life and its needs, as well as for pleasureful things that are unwarranted. Those who ask in faith for anything in particular should always submit their own will to the will of God. In our petitions we should pray with childlike faith and never cling stubbornly to our demands. We do not know what is truly necessary or good for us in temporal matters, but our heavenly Father does know. Thanksgiving lies in an understanding and knowledge of God's favor. It is an unfailing and steadfast turning of a good will to God even if at time there is no external giving of thanks, nor inner affection, or even if it be given in a sluggish way. The Apostle speaks of this when he says, 'The desire to do right is in me, but I do not find myself carrying through' (Romans 7:18). It is as if he were to say: willing is always there, but sometimes it lies hidden; it is ineffective, because I seek to carry out a good thing but I do not find it taking place. This is the charity which never fails (cf. 1 Corinthians 13:8); it is praying without ceasing and giving thanks, of which the Apostle says: 'Pray without ceasing' (1 Thessalonians 5:17), 'giving thanks always' (Ephesians 5:20)."

Rightly does the Lord say, "Until now you have not asked for anything in my name. Ask and you will receive and so your joy will be full." (Marcil, ed., *Sermones*, pp. 190–191)

Reflection

As Christians, we know that we should pray. Prayer is spending time with God, but this time can be of different qualities. Think of various ways in which one person can visit with another. In one situation, two people attempt to watch a blaring television while carrying on a conversation. In another scene, one of the two parties is wishing the visit were concluded so that the individual could return to some pressing but unfinished business. In the third scene, both parties are sincerely absorbed in the conversation. The phone must ring three times before either party really hears it, so deeply is each person concentrating full affection and attention on the other.

Our prayer life is sometimes like one of these scenes. We pray amid distractions, either mental or physical, to which we readily give our attention. Or we pray out of duty, not out of love, and breathe a sigh of relief when the prayer time is over, for now we can get on with the really "important" things. But if we pray with our whole soul and mind, our thoughts are focused on God. In this deep form of prayer, we share our deepest needs with God and ask for help, guidance, comfort, and healing. We dialog about our experiences honestly and forthrightly with the One who created us. We praise the One with whom we share. Then, when we have unburdened our soul, we pause and listen. And the voice of the Spirit begins to speak in the quiet of our spirit.

Anthony, like Jesus, tells us to pray, no matter how or in what circumstances. Prayer need not be more complicated than supplication, conversation, petition, and thanksgiving. God is always with us, waiting to enter into relationship.

✧ Reread Anthony's words on prayer. Then examine each of the prayer styles that he mentions.

✦ Do you ever try to know God's will without asking for the grace to hear and bear it?
✦ Concerning prayer, do you ever have a time of union with God when you can actually be present to God? If not, can you create this time?
✦ When you pray a prayer of petition, how willing are you to accept God's answer of "No, I have something better for you"?
✦ Is your thanksgiving cheerfully given? Do you agree with Anthony that we should give thanks even if we lack inner affection in doing so?

✧ Offer your supplications or petitions to God right now. Remind yourself that God is present, and then just begin. God listens.

✧ In a litany, a favorite hymn, a dance, or a spontaneous song, give thanks to God for all the blessings in your life.

✧ One type of prayer is the prayer of presence. In this prayer, one is simply present to God. Start by simply sitting still, listening to your breath. If you need help focusing, pray the name of Jesus with each inhalation and exhalation. At some point, let go of the name and just be still, knowing God is with you.

✧ Anthony frequently took one line of scripture, or even one phrase, and meditated on it; this form of prayer is called *lectio divina*. He would look for symbolic meanings in the words and relate them to God. Practice this by opening your Bible to one of the Gospels and choose one sentence. Read the sentence out loud over and over until you have memorized it *(meditatio)*. Then get comfortable and think about this sentence deeply *(ruminatio)*. What is the literal sense of the sentence? The symbolic sense? Does it relate to other passages of scripture? How? When you have completed your meditation, write in a journal the sentence, its scriptural reference, and what it means to you *(oratio)*. Frequent use of this process fosters contemplation.

✧ Contemplation is very close to what Anthony means by "prayer" in the previous reading. If you would like to receive this gift of "the expressly affectionate state of a person united to God," ask God to grant it to you. Anthony gives advice on how to achieve this.

> "You will not be able to see God if you do not listen obediently. If you are deaf, then you will be blind as well. Listen in obedience, then, with a heart full of love. Then you will be able to see God with the eye of contemplation, for it is written (Sirach 17:7): God implants his eye in his heart. God implants his eye in the human heart when the human person listens to God with his or her whole heart and when, therefore, God gives that person the light of contemplation" (Hardick, *He Came to You So That You Might Come to Him*, pp. 158–159)

> Ask God for the grace of contemplation.

✧ Praying with other people has power, too. From the earliest days of the church, Christians have prayed together. Who do you pray with? How do you or could you enrich your prayer life by praying with other people?

God's Word

There is no need to worry; but if there is anything you need, pray for it, asking God for it with prayer and thanksgiving, and that peace of God, which is so much greater than we can understand, will guard your hearts and your thoughts in Christ Jesus. (Adapted from Philippians 4:6–7)

Closing prayer: Pray Anthony's prayer:

Lord Jesus Christ,
may we sing your song of praise,
rejoice only in you,
live modestly,
abandon our worries,
and tell you all our needs,
so that in the refuge of your peace,
we can live in the kingdom of the celestial Jerusalem.
With your help
who are blessed and glorious for eternal ages. Amen.
(Jarmak, trans., Praise to You Lord, p. 38)

✧ Meditation 14 ✧

Joy

Theme: People want to be happy, but no one obtains joy by striving for it. Joy is a fruit of a life centered on God and an infallible sign of God's presence.

Opening prayer: Dear Jesus, you said, "I will see you again, and your hearts will rejoice, and no one will take your joy from you" (John 16:22). Let me know you, love you, trust you, and obey you with all my being so that my joy in you may be complete.

About Anthony

Unfortunately, in the holy paintings of modern times, Anthony is often portrayed with either a strong, almost severe expression or a gaze that can only be described as doleful, as if the artist attempted to blend holiness and sorrow. Such portrayals do Anthony an injustice for there is no indication that he was a severe or sorrowful saint.

Anthony spoke forcefully and pointedly against sin, but he also spoke enthusiastically of mercy. He could meditate deeply on the Passion of Christ and weep over the sins of the world, but the sorrow in these instances was engendered by the circumstances on which he meditated. From his biographies and his sermons, it is apparent that Anthony was a man filled with God's joy. His joy was the deep Biblical joy of knowing, loving, and serving God. Joy was not something Anthony sought. Rather, it was a fruit of his devotion to his Creator.

One of the most popular legends about Anthony shows how his joy came from doing God's will—in a most unexpected way. Anthony and his companion, Friar Ruggiero, had been preaching in Rimini for three months to audiences that were less than enthusiastic. While sitting by the sea, Ruggiero wondered how much longer the two should waste time on the people of Rimini. Anthony replied: "God will make known His will if we do not allow discouragement to overwhelm us, Ruggiero."

Then the legend takes an amazing turn:

The surface of the water had been calm and smooth, undisturbed by the minor breeze. Now the area before them and on either side puddled and rippled. At each of the puddles, a fish lifted its mouth from the water then slid gently back beneath the surface. On every side, fish thrust through the surface, then quietly retreated.

Antonio stood and approached the edge of the bluff. . . . Thousands of fish . . . seemed to wait. . . . These fish were as people who had come reverently to hear the word of God!

"Then hear the word of God!" Antonio cried out joyfully. "O fishes of the sea and of the river, hear the word of God these infidel[s] . . . refuse to hear!"

Antonio looked down on them curiously. . . . They remained quiet and motionless before him. Antonio knew a great, overwhelming joy.

While he preached to the creatures in the water before him, Antonio heard sounds behind him. Whispers and murmurs carried to him. Patiently, joyfully, he continued to extol to the dumb creatures the mercies of their Creator. Let these people who had hardened themselves against their God witness the adoration even the fishes of the sea paid to Him. . . . He raised his hand in blessing over the water, then watched the fish disappear beneath the surface.

. . . The families who had been laughing and talking were silent; the few had become fifty . . . who might open the path for the word of God to all the people of Rimini. (John E. Beahn, *A Rich Young Man: Saint Anthony of Padua*, pp. 187–188)

Pause: Where have you been looking for joy?

Anthony's Words

Joy is a state of being that comes, Anthony says, when we are humble enough to trust and to obey God. "If you, O man, heed God's commandments, you will be joyful and live in an unending peace." (Marcil, ed., *Sermones*, p. 147).

In his sermon for the fourth Sunday after Easter, he explained how joy and peace come:

> Christ had two quite different inheritances: one was from his mother, and this was struggle and sorrow; the other was from his Father, and this was joy and peace. From the fact that we are co-heirs with him we must accept the same double inheritance. We err if we expect to be favored with the second inheritance without the first, because God has planted the second one in the first, so that we would not seek the one without the other. He grafted the tree of life into the tree of knowledge of good and evil when "the Word became flesh" (John 1:14). Hence: "He will be like a tree planted near a running stream" (Psalm 1:3). And Isaiah: God "laid the earth's foundation and therein he planted the heavens" (51:16). In the earth of humanity, founded on the seven pillars of a sevenfold grace, he planted the heavens of the divinity. Let us, then, take possession of the first inheritance which Christ left us, so that we may deserve to come to the second. (Marcil, ed., *Sermones*, p. 171)

Reflection

Joy comes from knowing God's will and embracing it. God's will manifests itself through two "inheritances," namely "struggle and sorrow" and "joy and peace." Anthony's last sentence in the above reading bears repeating. "Let us, then, take possession of the first inheritance which Christ left us, so that we may deserve to come to the second." Only by embracing the struggle and sorrow of life according to Christ and by cooperating with God who turns everything to good will we know joy (cf. Romans 8:28).

God's will is embodied in Jesus' declaration: "You shall love the Lord your God with all your heart, and with all your soul, and with all your mind. This is the greatest and first commandment. And a second is like it: You shall love your neighbor as yourself" (Matthew 22:37–39).

How one is to love God and our neighbor varies from person to person. Anthony loved through his ministry and by spending time alone with God in prayer. We love through our actions and prayer. Time alone with God increases our love of God and also reveals God's will for us. Then, as Anthony said, "The doers of God's word are those who ask for the fullness of joy and receive it" (Marcil, ed., *Sermones*, p. 193).

✧ Reread "Anthony's Words" again, slowly. Pause to reflect on each word and sentence. Choose one sentence and repeat it over and over, pausing between each word. What is the Spirit speaking to you through these words?

✧ Anthony said, "If you . . . heed God's commandments, you will be joyful and live in an unending peace." Which of God's commandments do you find challenging to heed? How could you heed them better? Ask God for the grace you need to heed these commandments more fully.

✧ Anthony realized that joy does not come from avoiding sorrow, struggle, and suffering. Rather, joy comes when we live in harmony with God's will, when we harmonize with the demands of love. Ponder these questions:

◆ Are you willing to embrace the suffering and sorrow that commitment to life, love, and relationships bring, or do you prefer to struggle against them?

◆ Recall some instances in your life when you felt joy even in the midst of the messiness of life.

Ask God for the grace to embrace the hard edges of loving, and thank God for the joy you have been blessed with.

✧ Anthony had balance in his life. He served others, and he spent time alone with God. He tells us that joy comes by doing God's will in service to both God and neighbor. Examine your life. How do you serve God? Neighbor? Ask God to show you if what you are doing is God's will for you. Is your life out of balance? If you need to make some changes in your life, pray for the courage to do so.

✧ Do you know anyone who is joyful? Talk with him or her about the sources of joy.

God's Word

"I love you just as God has loved me. Stay in the embrace of my love by keeping my commandments. I tell you this so that my joy will dwell inside you and so your own joy may be full. This is my commandment: love one another just as I have loved all of you. No one has greater love than those who lay down their life for their friends. You are my friends if you keep my commandments." (Adapted from John 15:9–14)

Closing prayer: Pray Anthony's prayer:

Let us pray that the Lord Jesus Christ
pour his grace into us
by means of which we ask for and receive
the fullness of true joy.
May he ask the Father for us;
may he grant us true religion
so that we may merit
to come to the kingdom of eternal life.
May he grant this,
he who is to be praised,
the beginning and the end,
wonderful, ineffable for all ages.

(Marcil, ed., *Sermones*, p. 204)

✧ Meditation 15 ✧

Absorbed into the Light

Theme: Death can be a door that opens onto eternal life with God. Anthony reminded himself, his listeners, and reminds us that we have it within our will to choose our eternal destiny.

Opening prayer: God of life and God of death, help me live virtuously and build your reign so that I may come into the inheritance promised by Christ.

About Anthony

Anthony lived at a time when the hereafter was very real to his listeners. Life was short and difficult. Illnesses considered easily curable today decimated populations. Death came often and proved hard to ignore. Even the most sinful and self-indulgent characters believed in heaven and hell and would frequently send for a priest on their deathbed, in hope of having their sins remitted so that they might escape eternal damnation by the skin of their teeth.

Anthony was aware of this prevailing attitude, and a major thrust of his sermons was to have his listeners repent now and live a life of holy reform in anticipation of heavenly reward. Those who did not reform, he was swift to point out, were on their way to perdition. Anthony drives home this point again and again in his sermons.

So forceful was he that the following legend is told about him. Anthony was asked to preach at a notorious usurer's funeral. Instead of offering only honey-coated, consoling platitudes, Anthony emphasized to the mourners that the man was buried in hell because, for all his life, his heart lay not with Christ but with his money. He made such an impression on his audience that one of the number did an autopsy on the corpse and indeed found it to be without a heart. Whereupon the amateur physician searched among the man's store of coins and found the heart, still warm, among them.

Anthony, who had devoted his life to Christ, was totally at peace when God called him home. This is evident in the last recorded moments of Anthony's earthly existence.

> Once he found himself with the friars at Arcella, the hand of the Lord weighed heavier on him and, as the malady grew more violent, he showed signs of intense anguish. When he had rested for a brief moment, having confessed and received absolution, he began to sing a hymn to the glorious Virgin, saying, "O glorious Lady," etc.
>
> Having finished the hymn, he suddenly raised his eyes toward heaven and, with a stunned look, stared in front of himself for a long time. When the friar who was supporting him asked what he saw, he answered, "I see my Lord."
>
> The friars who were present, seeing that his happy end was approaching, decided to anoint the saint of God with the oil of holy unction. When a certain friar came to him, carrying the sacred oil as usual, blessed Anthony looked straight at him and said, "Brother, it is not necessary to do this to me, for I already have this anointing within me. Nonetheless, it is good for me and I agree to it." And, having extended his hands and then joined his palms, he sang the penitential psalms with the friars until he completed them to the end. He still held up for almost half an hour. Then, that most holy soul, freed from the prison of his flesh, was absorbed into the abyss of light. (Przewozny, trans., "*Assidua*," pp. 24–25)

Pause: Ask yourself, Am I ready to die?

Anthony's Words

"Mary stood outside of the tomb weeping. As she wept, she stooped down and looked into the tomb. She saw two angels in white, seated, one at the head, and one at the feet, where the body of Jesus had been placed" (John 20:11–12). Now pay attention to these words: "The burial place is called a tomb or 'monument' because it ad'mon'ishes us 'ment'ally (mon-ment) to be mindful of the dead." It signifies, thus, the remembrance of our own death and burial, which two are a constant admonition to us to have heartfelt sorrow and to apply ourselves to works of penance. "Mary," therefore, "stood at the monument," because she stood, humble and inwardly turned, remembering her own death, so that if the Lord were to come he might find her vigilant (cf. Luke 12:37). In what way did she stand? The gospel says: "Outside, weeping." Outside, not inside; for outside there is nothing else but "weeping and much loud lamenting." "Rachel," i.e. the simple penitent soul—note, the name Rachel means sheep—"weeps over her children," i.e. her deeds, which having been created in sin were dead. "And she refused to be consoled because they were no more" (Matthew 2:18); they were so enjoyable alive, but now they are gone. Oh, it is so easy to sink down low, but so hard to ascend again. "What took so long to be born slips away so quickly." "As she wept, she stooped down, and looked into the monument." Here is the humility of a real penitent. Note the three phrases: she wept, she stooped, she looked into. To weep is to show contrition; to stoop is to go to confession; to look into is to make amends. To this last one a person turns intently when he directs his attention to the monument of his death. (Marcil, ed., *Sermones*, pp. 69–70)

Reflection

When someone we love dies, particularly if the death is sudden or unexpected, we are tempted to think that God is being unfair. Death should not have happened, at least not now. Even when an elderly or terminally ill person dies, we tend to view death as an intrusion rather than as a normal part of life.

Anthony wanted his listeners to think about death, not because he was morbid, but because he saw the big picture. Those who went through earthly life without reforming their life were, to use a modern analogy, like those who knew they were about to go on a plane trip to an exotic tropical paradise, but never troubled themselves to buy the tickets. When the flight departed, they were left behind. If Anthony lived today, he would want everyone to be on board, and he would remind us that the time to purchase the tickets is now.

Anthony would also remind us that reform must come from within and extend into our actions. Even though he accepted the anointing, he said, "I already have this anointing within me." The exterior ritual means little if the soul is not burning for God—repentant, grateful, loving, and anointed.

✧ Reread "Anthony's Words." Then ask yourself:
✦ Do I have "this anointing within me"?
✦ How can I approach death with hope and acceptance?
✦ If Jesus were to give the homily at my funeral, what would he say?

✧ Ponder and pray over this statement by Henry David Thoreau in *Walden*—a statement similar to those made by writers throughout the ages: "I wished to live deliberately . . . and not, when I came to die, discover that I had not lived. I did not wish to live what was not life" (pp. 1279–1280).

Then reflect on what Jesus said, "I came that [you] may have life, and have it abundantly" (John 10:10). Dialog with Jesus about this question: How can I live my life fully, so that when I come to die, I will know that I have lived now and will live in the next life?

✧   Pray over each of these questions.

✦ Have you told your family what you want done when you approach death?

✦ How do you feel about artificial life support? Organ donation? A full funeral? An open casket? Cremation? Burial?

✦ What would you want in your obituary or your eulogy?

✦ Have you made a will?

✦ How do you feel about this list of questions?

✧   Recall the passing of a loved one. Ponder the good about her or him. Give thanks to God for this loved one and ask for the graces you need to emulate the good in this special person.

✧   Visit someone who is terminally ill. Do not attempt to offer simple platitudes about the person's condition or future. Simply be present, listen, and, if the person is willing, pray together. Ask that Jesus become fully real to both of you through this illness.

✧   Does your church or community have a hospice program in place to care for the dying? Consider becoming a volunteer visitor for such a program. If there are no hospice programs in your church or community, what could be done to begin one?

God's Word

When sin had you enslaved, righteousness had no hold on you. So what did you gain from a life enslaved? The fruit of sin is only death. Now you are freed from sin and bound to God. Holiness is the fruit of this new life. Eternal life is assured. The payoff of sin is death. God freely gives eternal life through Christ our Savior. (Adapted from Romans 6:20–23)

Closing prayer: Pray Anthony's prayer:

We beg you, Unity and Trinity,
that the soul which you have created
may safely flee to you
on that last day of affliction and fire,
when the silver rope will be broken.
Welcome it, that freed
from the snares of evil,
it may come to you with the freedom
and glory of a child of God.
With your help,
one God in three,
who are blessed for all ages. Amen.

(Jarmak, trans., *Praise to You Lord*, p. 6)

F·O·R·G·I·V·E·N·E·S·S

✧ For Further Reading ✧

Anthony of Padua. *Praise to You Lord: Prayers of St. Anthony.* Trans. Claude Jarmak. Padua, Italy: Prov. Pad. F.M.C. Editrice Grafiche Messaggero di S. Antonio, 1986.*

————. *Herald of the Good News.* Trans. Claude Jarmak. Ellicott City, MD: Conventual Franciscan Friars, 1995.

————. *Seek First His Kingdom.* Ed. Livio Poloniato. Padua, Italy: Prov. Pad. F.M.C. Editrice Grafiche Messaggero di S. Antonio, 1988.

————. Sermones *for the Easter Cycle.* Ed. George Marcil. St. Bonaventure, NY: Franciscan Institute, 1994.

Beahn, John E. *A Rich Young Man: Saint Anthony of Padua.* 1953. Reprint, Ellicott City, MD: Companions of St. Anthony, 1995.

Clasen, Sophronius. *St. Anthony: Doctor of the Church.* Trans. Ignatius Brady. Chicago: Franciscan Herald Press, 1973.**

Gamboso, Vergilio. *St. Anthony of Padua: His Life and Teaching.* Trans. H. Partridge. Padua, Italy: Prov. Pad. F.M.C. Messaggero di S. Antonio—Editrice, 1991.*

Hardick, Lothar. *Anthony of Padua: Proclaimer of the Gospel.* Trans. Zachary Hayes and Jason M. Miskuly. Ed. Cassian A. Miles and Janet E. Gianopoulos. Paterson, NJ: St. Anthony's Guild, 1993.

————. *He Came to You So That You Might Come to Him: The Life and Teaching of St. Anthony of Padua.* Trans. Zachary Hayes. Chicago: Franciscan Herald Press, 1989.**

*These books are available from the Anthonian Association, 101 Anthony Drive, Mount St. Francis, IN 47146.

**These books are available from the Franciscan Press, Quincy University, 1800 College Avenue, Quincy, IL 62301-2699.

Nugent, Madeline Pecora. *St. Anthony: Words of Fire, Life of Light*. Boston: Pauline Books and Media, 1995.

Przewozny, Bernard, trans. *Life of St. Anthony: "Assidua."* Padua, Italy: Prov. Pad. F.M.C. Editrice Grafiche Messaggero di S. Antonio, 1984.*

Purcell, Mary. *Saint Anthony and His Times*. Garden City, NY: Hanover House, 1959.

Stoddard, Charles Warren. *Saint Anthony: The Wonder Worker of Padua*. Rockford, IL: Tan Books, 1971.

Acknowledgments *(continued)*

The psalm on page 49 is from *Psalms Anew: In Inclusive Language,* compiled by Nancy Schreck and Maureen Leach (Winona, MN: Saint Mary's Press, 1986). Copyright © 1986 by Saint Mary's Press. All rights reserved.

The scriptural material found on pages 32, 35, 37–38, 41, 55, 59, 72, 81, 82, 88–89, 95, 102, 108, and 113 is freely adapted and is not to be understood or used as an official translation of the Bible.

All other scriptural quotations used in this book are from the New Revised Standard Version of the Bible. Copyright © 1989 by the Division of Christian Education of the National Council of the Churches of Christ in the United States of America. Used with permission. All rights reserved.

The excerpts on pages 27, 29–30, 32, 40, 42–43, 45–46, 47, 49, 51–52, 55, 57–58, 79–80, 83, 86, and 92 are from *Seek First His Kingdom,* edited by Livio Poloniato, OFM Conv (Padua, Italy: Prov. Pad. F.M.C. Editrice Grafiche Messaggero di S. Antonio, 1988), pages 11, 32–34, 33, 174–175, 171, 60–61, 147, 135–136, 133–134, 136, 118, 82, 172, 156–157, and 159–160, respectively. Copyright © 1988 by Prov. Pad. F.M.C. Editrice Grafiche Messaggero di S. Antonio. Used with permission.

The excerpt on page 29 is from "The First Life of St. Francis," by Thomas of Celano, in *St. Francis of Assisi, Writings and Early Biographies: English Omnibus of the Sources for the Life of St. Francis,* edited by Marion A. Habig, OFM (Quincy, IL: Franciscan Press, 1991), pages 269–270. Copyright © 1991 by Franciscan Press. Used with permission.

The excerpt on page 34 is from *Anthony of Padua: Proclaimer of the Gospel,* by Lothar Hardick, OFM, translated by Zachary Hayes, OFM, and Jason Miskuly, OFM, edited by Cassian A. Miles, OFM, and Janet E. Gianopoulos (Paterson, NJ: St. Anthony's Guild, 1993), insert. Copyright © 1993 by Corinne Abbazia Hekker NYC. Reprinted with permission of The Franciscans, St. Anthony's Guild, Paterson, NJ 07509-2948.

The excerpts on pages 34–35 and 67–68 are from *Saint Anthony Messenger,* May 1986 and October 1989, page 4 of each issue.

The excerpts by Vergilio Gamboso on page 61 are from *St. Anthony of Padua: His Life and Teaching*, translated by H. Partridge (Padua, Italy: Prov. Pad. F.M.C. Messaggero di S. Antonio—Editrice, 1991), pages 140 and 130. Copyright © 1991 by Prov. Pad. F.M.C. Messaggero di S. Antonio—Editrice.

The excerpts on pages 61–62, 97–98, 105, 105, 106, 108, and 111 are from *Anthony of Padua: "Sermones" for the Easter Cycle*, edited by George Marcil, OFM (St. Bonaventure, NY: Franciscan Institute, 1994), pages 95, 190–191, 147, 171, 193, 204, and 69–70. Copyright © 1994 by the Franciscan Institute of St. Bonaventure University. Used with permission.

The hymn on page 63, "O Gloriosa Domina!" is an original translation by Geoffrey Chase, done at the personal request of the author.

The excerpt on pages 69–70 is a paraphrase from *Whatever Became of Sin?* by Karl Menninger (New York: Bantam Books, 1978). Copyright © 1973 by Karl Menninger.

The excerpt on page 79 is from *Life of St. Anthony of Padua*, by Ubaldus da Rieti, OSF (Boston: Angel Guardian Press, 1895), pages 90–91.

The excerpt on pages 104–105 is from *A Rich Young Man: Saint Anthony of Padua*, by John E. Beahn (Reprint, Ellicott City, MD: Companions of St. Anthony, 1995), pages 186–188. Copyright © 1953 by the Bruce Publishing Company.

The excerpt on page 112 is from *Walden*, by Henry David Thoreau, in *The American Tradition in Literature*, 4th ed., edited by Sculley Bradley, Richmond Croom Beatty, E. Hudson Long, and George Perkins (n.p.: Grosset and Dunlap, 1974), 1:1279–1280. Copyright © 1974 by Grosset and Dunlap.

Titles in the Companions for the Journey Series

Praying with Anthony of Padua

Praying with Benedict   forthcoming

Praying with Catherine McAuley

Praying with Catherine of Siena

Praying with Clare of Assisi

Praying with Dominic

Praying with Dorothy Day

Praying with Elizabeth Seton

Praying with Francis of Assisi

Praying with Hildegard of Bingen

Praying with Ignatius of Loyola

Praying with John Baptist de La Salle

Praying with John of the Cross

Praying with Julian of Norwich

Praying with Louise de Marillac

Praying with Teresa of Ávila

Praying with Thérèse of Lisieux

Praying with Thomas Merton

Praying with Vincent de Paul

Order from your local religious bookstore or from

Saint Mary's Press
702 TERRACE HEIGHTS
WINONA MN 55987-1320
USA
1-800-533-8095